SELECTIONS

from the first two issues of
The New York Review of Books

Edited by
Robert B. Silvers and Barbara Epstein

SELECTIONS
from the first two issues
of *The New York Review of Books*

The New York Review of Books
Rea S. Hederman, Publisher
Robert B. Silvers and Barbara Epstein, Editors

For subscription information please write to
Michael Johnson, Subscription Manager
The New York Review of Books
1755 Broadway, 5th floor
New York, NY 10019-3780

Design by Andrea Barash

Table of Contents

Introduction

by Elizabeth Hardwick

Twenty-five years have gone by since the first appearance of *The New York Review of Books*.

In December 1962 there was an extended strike that halted publication of *The New York Times*. The *Times* was, and is, a national addiction of the severest kind and symptoms of distress were acute during the stoppage. The lack of news was the greatest deprivation, but a blank in the coverage of the arts, especially those of performance, could mean oblivion. Books fortunately exist after the curtain goes down, the publication date often being nothing more than a handiness for commerce. Still, there was a spot, a vacancy, in the matter of comment on books, and the group that organized *The New York Review*, including its present editors, edged, jumped—whatever you like—into it. The first issue was published in February, the second in April, and the *Review* started regular biweekly publication in September.

A selection from the first two special issues is offered here— a bit of archival material from the pages and pages of the years.

Edmund Wilson's interview with himself. F.W. Dupee's reflections on *The Fire Next Time* by James Baldwin, Norman Mailer on Hemingway, Richard Wilbur on Longfellow, and the other selections reprinted here give an idea of what was first presented to the public concerned with books and ideas. These were written a long, or is it a short?, time ago, and many cultural dramas have reached the stage since. The present and the past as they endure in serious books, in art, and in world events were the mission of *The New York Review* and remain so.

Looking over the early issues one can see that they are not the beginning stages of some Darwinian or organic process. It is the nature of such an enterprise to be a flow rather than a curve or even an adaptation. Changing subject matter itself is the internal mutation of all magazines, with each issue a birth or a rebirth as one sees it.

To meditate upon the reviews of books is to wonder if there is not something peculiarly stubborn, even out-of-date, about those among us who write the books and those who write about them. Years of scholarship that still show a kind of monkish tenacity and dedication, years of prodding the imagination in fiction and poetry, years of confinement in the prison of historical events—and years to earn the authority to compose a relevant examination of the themes that make up the dramas of current and past culture. So *The New York Review* may be thought of as a service to the doggedness of writers and to the fidelity of those who continue to publish them.

The term "book review" for a publication may be as wide or as narrow a designation as the editors and the audience desire. *The New York Review* is a journal of criticism. Criticism itself is not a precise engagement, unless one wants to see it as one of many unfortunate parental assumptions, or presumptions. In reality, it encounters a work of art, a construction of scholarship, an arrangement of opinions , an event in the historical or intellectual world. Without the exercise of this faculty art and the record of thought would cease to signify, would drop into a void. Opinions write books and opinions write about books. But opinion is never stable, never under the protection of some minor deity. That can be seen in the vehement, space-filling letter columns of the *Review*, those engagements between the defendant and the prosecutor that might go on forever without a verdict were it not for new contests on the docket in the next issue.

As a part of what is called, with resignation or concern, our "service economy," the *Review* is nevertheless hardly to be termed a fast fix. I find that an article in one of the very recent issues was given to the large volumes of *The Cambridge History of Latin America*, an undertaking as suitably abundant in facts and ideas as the vast, compelling continent itself. The elucidation of such a work can scarcely be a brief notice with a whiff of opinion in a coda.

I notice that the drawings of David Levine appeared first in the third issue of the magazine. The first portrait, if I understand it, was a sort of generic drawing of a scruffy-haired man at his typewriter—and looking in the mirror. Not Everyman, but perhaps a hint of Everyman when he is a writer. Levine's visions of personages living and dead have been a bonus of each issue. Somehow he mysteriously commands the talent to catch in the frame a recognizable face and a sly comment upon the work, a kind of judging of value or lack of it, a hint of the dilemmas and achievements of thousands of public figures.

Twenty-five years is a moderate celebration, a silver anniversary, a certainly agreeable accumulation. In the history of American magazines longevity is more remarkable than the contrary. Once established a name seems to fix itself in the landscape with the frank insistence of stones and mortar. The old Transcendentalist publication, *The Dial*, was offered to the public in 1840 by Emerson and Margaret Fuller. It went into a sort of cold storage, but remained in the national memory and was revived and finally after the high editorship of Marianne Moore expired in 1929. *The North American Review*, edited at various times by Henry Adams and Charles Eliot Norton, lives on today as a literary magazine published in the northwest. *The New York Review* for its part is still at the stage where it is growing both in pages and the size of its audience, which now includes thousands of readers in Europe, Africa, and Asia.

In 1963 Kennedy was president and in 1988 a new president is to be elected, an occasion of much weight and a noticeable amount of weightlessness, like that of beings orbiting in space. As a cultural paper *The New York Review* exists in its time. In a sense all events past and present move under a layer of books written, books that are a record of similarities, sometimes dismaying and sometimes consoling, and of upstart diversions always waiting to be measured for size. *The New York Review* tries to go beyond mere reaction to books and has itself become, every two weeks, something like a short book on the state of the culture and the world.

—*Elizabeth Hardwick,*
on the occasion of the Review's
twenty-fifth anniversary, 1988

James Baldwin and the "Man"

by F. W. Dupee

As a writer of polemical essays on the Negro question James Baldwin has no equals. He probably has, in fact, no real competitors. The literary role he has taken on so deliberately and played with so agile an intelligence is one that no white writer could possibly imitate and that few Negroes, I imagine, would wish to embrace in toto. Baldwin impresses me as being the Negro *in extremis,* a virtuoso of ethnic suffering, defiance, and aspiration. His role is that of the man whose complexion constitutes his fate, and not only in a society poisoned by prejudice but, it sometimes seems, in general. For he appears to have received a heavy dose of existentialism; he is at least half-inclined to see the Negro question in the light of the Human Condition. So he wears his color as Hester Prynne did her scarlet letter, proudly. And like her he converts this thing, in itself so absurdly material, into a form of consciousness, a condition of spirit. Believing himself to have been branded as different from and inferior to the white majority, he will make a virtue of his situation. He will *be* different and in his own way be better.

His major essays—for example, those collected in *Notes of a Native Son*—show the extent to which he is able to be different and in his own way better. Most of them were written, as other such pieces generally are, for the magazines, some obviously on assignment. And their subjects—a book, a person, a locale, an encounter—are the inevitable subjects of magazine essays. But Baldwin's way with them is far from inevitable. To apply criticism "in depth" to *Uncle Tom's Cabin* is, for him, to illuminate not only a book, an author, an age, but a whole strain in a country's culture. Similarly with those routine themes, the Paris expatriate and Life With Father, which he treats in "Equal In Paris" and the title piece of *Notes of a Native Son,* and which he wholly transfigures. Of course the transfiguring process in Baldwin's essays owes something to the fact that the point of view is a Negro's, an outsider's, just as the satire of American manners in *Lolita* and *Morte d'Urban* depends on their being written from the angle of, respectively, a foreign-born creep and a Catholic priest. But Baldwin's point of view in his essays is not merely that of the generic Negro. It is, as I have said, that of a highly stylized Negro, a role which he plays with an artful and zestful consistency and which he expresses in a language distinguished by clarity, brevity, and a certain formal elegance. He is in love, for example, with syntax, with sentences that mount through clearly articulated stages to a resounding and clarifying climax and then gracefully subside. For instance this one, from *The Fire Next Time:*

> Girls, only slightly older than I was, who sang in the choir or taught Sunday school, the children of holy parents, underwent, before my eyes, their incredible metamorphosis, of which the most bewildering aspect was not their budding breasts or their rounding behinds but something deeper and more subtle, in their eyes, their heat, their odor, and the inflection of their voices.

Nobody else in democratic America writes sentences like this anymore. It suggests the ideal prose of an ideal literary community, some aristocratic France of one's dreams. This former Harlem boy has undergone his own incredible metamorphosis.

His latest book, *The Fire Next Time,* differs in important

ways from his earlier work in the essay. Its subjects are less concrete, less clearly defined; to a considerable extent he has exchanged prophecy for criticism, exhortation for analysis, and the results for his mind and style are in part disturbing. *The Fire Next Time* gets its title from a slave song: "God gave Noah the rainbow sign,/No more water the fire next time." But this small book with the incendiary title consists of two independent essays, both in the form of letters. One is a brief affair entitled "My Dungeon Shook" and addressed to "My Nephew on the One Hundredth Anniversary of the Emancipation." The ominous promise of this title is fulfilled in the text. Between the hundred-year-old anniversary and the fifteen-year-old nephew the disparity is too great even for a writer of Baldwin's rhetorical powers. The essay reads like some specimen of "public speech" as practiced by MacLeish or Norman Corwin. It is not good Baldwin.

The other, much longer, much more significant essay appeared first in a pre-Christmas number of *The New Yorker,* where it made, understandably, a sensation. It is called "Down At the Cross; Letter From a Region of My Mind." The subtitle should be noted. Evidently the essay is to be taken as only a partial or provisional declaration on Baldwin's part, a single piece of his mind. Much of it, however, requires no such appeal for caution on the reader's part. Much of it is unexceptionably first-rate. For example, the reminiscences of the writer's boyhood, which form the lengthy introduction. Other of Baldwin's writings have made us familiar with certain aspects of his Harlem past. Here he concentrates on quite different things: the boy's increasing awareness of the abysmally narrow world of choice he inhabits as a Negro, his attempt to escape a criminal existence by undergoing a religious conversion and becoming at fifteen a revivalist preacher, his discovery that he must learn to "inspire fear" if he hopes to survive the fear inspired in him by "the man"—the white man.

In these pages we come close to understanding why he eventually assumed his rather specialized literary role. It seems to have grown naturally out of his experience of New York City. As distinct from a rural or small-town Negro boy, who is early and firmly taught his place, young Baldwin knew the treacherous fluidity and anonymity of the metropolis, where hidden taboos and unpredictable animosities lay in wait for him and a trip to the 42nd Street Library could be a grim adventure. All this part of the book is perfect; and when Baldwin finally gets to what is his ostensible subject, the Black Muslims or Nation of Islam movement, he is very good too. As good, that is, as possible considering that his relations with the movement seem to have been slight. He once shared a television program with Malcolm X, "the movement's second-in-command," and he paid a brief and inconclusive visit to the first-in-command, the Honorable Elijah Muhammad, and his entourage at the party's headquarters in Chicago. (Muhammad ranks as a prophet; to him the Black Muslim doctrines were "revealed by Allah Himself.") Baldwin reports the Chicago encounter in charming detail and with what looks like complete honesty. On his leaving the party's rather grand quarters, the leader insisted on providing him with a car and driver to protect him "from the white devils until he gets wherever it is he is going." Baldwin accepted, he tells us, adding wryly: "I was, in fact, going to have a drink with several white devils on the other side of town."

He offers some data on the Black Muslim movement, its aims and finances. But he did a minimum of homework here. Had he done more he might at least have provided a solid base for the speculative fireworks the book abounds in. To cope thoroughly with the fireworks in short space, or perhaps any space, seems impossible. Ideas shoot from the book's pages as the sparks fly upward, in bewildering quantity and at random. I don't mean that it is all dazzle. On the cruel paradoxes of the Negro's life, the failures of Christianity, the relations of Negro and Jew, Baldwin is often superb. But a lot of damage is done to his argument by his indiscriminate raids on Freud, Lawrence, Sartre, Genet, and other psychologists, metaphysicians, and melodramatists. Still more damage is done by his refusal to draw on anyone so humble as Martin Luther King and his fellow-practitioners of non-violent struggle.

For example: "White Americans do not believe in death, and this is why the darkness of my skin so intimidates them." But suppose one or two white Americans are *not* intimidated. Suppose someone coolly asks what it means to "believe in death." Again: "Do I really *want* to be integrated into a burning house?" Since you have no other, yes; and the better-disposed firemen will welcome your assistance. Again: "A vast amount of the energy that goes into what we call the Negro problem is produced by the white man's profound desire not to be judged by those who are not white." You exaggerate the white man's consciousness of the Negro. Again: "The real reason that non-violence is considered to be a virtue in Negroes...is that white men do not want their lives, their self-image, or their property threatened." Of course they don't, especially their lives. Moreover, this imputing of "real reasons" for the behavior of entire populations is self-defeating, to put it mildly. One last quotation, this time a regular apocalypse:

> In order to survive as a human, moving, moral weight in the world, America and all the Western nations will be forced to reexamine themselves and release themselves from many things that are now taken to be sacred, and to discard nearly all the assumptions that have been used to justify their lives and their anguish and their crimes so long.

Since whole cultures have never been known to "discard nearly all their assumptions" and yet remain intact, this amounts to saying that any essential improvement in Negro-white relations, and thus in the quality of American life, is unlikely.

So much for the fireworks. What damage, as I called it, do they do to the writer and his cause—which is also the concern of plenty of others? When Baldwin replaces criticism with prophecy, he manifestly weakens his grasp of his role, his style, and his great theme itself. And to what end? Who is likely to be moved by such arguments, unless it is the more literate Black Muslims, whose program Baldwin specifically rejects as both vindictive and unworkable? And with the situation as it is in Mississippi and elsewhere—dangerous, that is, to the Negro struggle and the whole social order—is not a writer of Baldwin's standing obliged to submit his assertions to some kind of pragmatic test, some process whereby their truth or untruth will be gauged according to their social utility? He writes: "The Negroes of this country may never be able to rise to power, but they are very well placed indeed to precipitate chaos and ring down the curtain on the American dream." I should think that the anti-Negro extremists were even better placed than the Negroes to precipitate chaos, or at least to cause a lot of trouble; and it is unclear to me how *The Fire Next Time,* in its madder moments, confuses the latter. Assuming that a *book* can do anything to either.

To the Whitehouse

by Dwight Macdonald

Of the twenty essays here, written between 1949 and 1960 for a spectrum ranging from *Partisan Review* down to the *Saturday Evening Post*, six seemed to me excellent, nine poor, and five so-so. Quality was in inverse ratio to length and ambitiousness. Of the good ones, two are reportage: "Varieties of Communist Experience," about a month's trip in Russia, Poland, and Yugoslavia, and "Invasion of Europe, Family Style," a *feuilleton* carried off with style in a mere six pages. Four are polemics: "The Causes of the Civil War"; "The Statistical Soldier," a debunking of "social science" via a review of a two-volume work he describes as "a ponderous demonstration in Newspeak of such facts as these: new recruits do not like non-coms; front-line troops resent rear-echelon troops; married privates are more likely than single privates to worry about their families back home"; "The Politics of Nostalgia," the best brief exposé I know of the pretensions of the Buckley-Kirk "new conservatives" to either the noun or the adjective; and a fine deflation of John Osborne's *Look Back in Anger* as social criticism—and as drama. The five so-so pieces make up section three ("Men and Ideas") and deal with Reinhold Niebuhr, Walter Lippmann, Bernard DeVoto, Whittaker Chambers, and J. Robert Oppenheimer. They are long—half the book—and disappointing; much intelligent comment but neither the Men nor the Ideas are very interesting.

When he is not confronted with a polemical subject that

makes his style taut and forces him to think (which he can do when he has to), Schlesinger likes to slip into something more comfortable. His judgments tend to become official and reverential and to be expressed in the orotundities of the hardened public speaker. The conclusion of his essay on Niebuhr, for instance:

> If his searching realism gave new strength to American liberal democracy, or, rather, renewed sources of strength which had been too often neglected in the generations since the American Revolution, his own life and example have shown in compelling terms the possibilities of human contrition and human creativity within the tragedy of history.

The intonations of the fashionable preacher blend into those of the ideological con man—"human contrition" and "the tragedy of history" indeed! The last paragraph of the long piece on DeVoto (and why such labors over that middlebrow?) also makes me queasy:

> This was, as DeVoto saw it, the meaning of democracy. And fighting such a battle, DeVoto might have added, vindicates democracy by producing men of compassion, of courage and of faith. These men justify the battle and renew the strength and decency of a civilization. Bernard DeVoto was such a man.

That dying fall! That cant! These qualities are even more pronounced in the remaining essays, which are mostly political. Here the author's yea-saying, true-believer aspect emerges most clearly.

Schlesinger made his reputation with *The Age of Jackson*, which I thought at the time turgidly written and structurally confused. But the time was 1946 and the liberals—having just lost Roosevelt and gotten Truman—were understandably

worried. *The Age of Jackson* reassured them: it gave a rosy picture of Jacksonian democracy (myself, I see it as the first big
turning-point downward away from our political golden age—
the Jefferson-Madison period) and, more important, implied a
parallel with the New Deal. The results were a Pulitzer Prize
and Schlesinger's emergence as the scholarly (Professor of
History at Harvard) spokesman for what he was later to call,
flatteringly, the Vital Center—or, more prosaically, the
liberal-Northern wing of the Democratic Party. He became its
Virgil—all the more speedily because he was a facile and copious journalist—but a Virgil whose Augustus was in exile. He
was active, as speech writer and adviser, in the 1952 and 1956
Stevenson campaigns, and he wrote his *Aeneid*: the three-
volume *The Age of Roosevelt*, which provided for future
Democratic administrations the same historical-mythological
underpinning as the *Aeneid*, which Virgil hoped "would com-
memorate the glory of Rome and his friend, the Emperor
Augustus, and win back the Roman people to their primitive
religion and ancient virtues" (Magill: *Encyclopaedia of World
Authors*). Or, as the *Encyclopaedia Britannica* puts it: "The
problem was to compose a work of art which should represent
a great action of the heroic age and should also embody the
most vital ideas and sentiments of the hour." After his two dis-
appointments with Stevenson, Schlesinger shifted his alle-
giance to Kennedy some time before the 1960 convention. (I
imply no censure: Stevenson was politically dead after 1956
and rightly so: he had trimmed his sails but had capsized any-
way.) And so at last, after a decade of frustration, Schlesinger
became a Special Assistant, in the White House, to an
American President. The present book is mainly interesting
for the clues it gives to his political thinking.

The title comes from Emerson, a sage almost everybody
but me seems to find sagacious, who, in one of those capsule
Gems of Thought he specialized in, saw "mankind" as divided

between the party of conservatism-past-memory and the party of innovation-future-hope. If I had to choose between these Procrustean simplicities, I would choose the former. But I don't have to and so I don't. Neither does Schlesinger, but he does. His introduction, which for some reason is *not* dated "The White House, 1962," is the triumphal chant of the prophet who, after seven-plus lean years, sees his people liberated from the Egyptian bondage of the Eisenhower administrations:

> We no longer seem an old nation, tired, complacent and self-righteous. We no longer suppose that our national salvation depends on stopping history in its tracks and freezing the world in its present mold. Our national leadership is young, vigorous, intelligent, civilized and experimental.... We are Sons of Liberty once again.... We have awakened as from a trance.... The peculiarities of the fifties have almost the air of a forgotten nightmare.

He ends with an Emersonian Gem: "Freedom is inseparable from struggle; it is a process, not a conclusion."

The first two essays are "On Heroic Leadership and the Dilemma of Strong Men and Weak Peoples" (1960) and "The Decline of Greatness" (1958). The mere titles reveal a yearning which is a bit surprising in such a dedicated liberal and democrat, a desire which one assumes by now has been satiated by the President and his Attorney General, who are Heroic Leaders if ever there have been such, willing nay eager to assume "the Promethean responsibility to affirm human freedom against the supposed inevitabilities of history" and to "combat the infection of fatalism which might otherwise paralyze mass democracy." My view is that "mass democracy" is as much a contradiction in terms as was Hitler's "national socialism," but let it pass as an anarchist vagary. I cannot let pass, however, a sentence on page 17: "While the Executive should wield all his powers under the constitution with energy, he should not be able to abrogate the constitution except in face of war, revolution or economic chaos." True that the sainted Lincoln did suspend *habeas corpus* and when the Chief Justice of the United States freed a Southern sympathizer on the ground he had been illegally arrested, kept the prisoner in jail nonetheless, observing, "Justice Tawney has made his ruling. Now let him enforce it"—an aside all too reminiscent of Stalin's famous query as to how many divisions the Pope commanded. Also true that Wilson and Franklin Roosevelt cut a few corners in wartime—and why is it always the great liberal presidents who do these things? Maybe because they have good consciences, supplied by intellectuals like Mr. Schlesinger. But even a liberal Northern Democrat might be given pause by the above formulation; he might think these wartime abrogations of the Constitution were shameful and against his principles; he might remember that, except for Lincoln, no president, even in wartime, has openly "abrogated the constitution," although our author takes it as a matter of course; and he might also remember that no president so far has abrogated the Constitution on the plea of "economic chaos," and wonder why Schlesinger should give away in advance, nay even suggest, such an invasion of our constitutional rights. In fact, he might have disturbing thoughts about Heroic Leadership and about the part played by liberalistic ideologues like Arthur Schlesinger, Jr., in justifying such illiberal, not to say unconstitutional, tactics even before the Heroic Leaders themselves have attempted them.

In "*Time* and the Intellectuals," Schlesinger sneers at Henry Luce for demanding from writers positive and noncritical attitudes toward American institutions: "Those intellectuals who have faith in *Time*'s America and are ready to denounce their colleagues for criticizing it are, in *Time*'s valuable phrase, Men of Affirmation. The Men of Protest are a disgruntled collection of snobs, grouches and expatriates, grumbling and griping in the outer darkness." He goes on to speak in eloquent and convincing terms of "the historical role of American intellectuals" as essentially one of protest. He was writing in 1956, when Eisenhower was in the White House, but now we have a different occupant and our author sings a different tune. "We need more people who don't give a damn and can awaken responses in us," Schlesinger wrote in 1956. But the basic quality needed to be a Special Assistant to the President is that one does give a damn. I wish my friend Arthur Schlesinger, Jr., who is, as they say, "once you get to know him," a witty, clever, sensible, and decent fellow, had never gotten involved with high politics.

Buenos Aires

by Robert Lowell

In my room at the Hotel Continental
a thousand miles from nowhere,
I heard
the bulky, beefy breathing of the herds.

Cattle furnished my new clothes:
my coat of limp, chestnut-colored suede,
my sharp shoes
that hurt my toes.

A false fin de siècle *decorum*
snored over Buenos Aires,
lost in the pampas
and run by the barracks.

Old strong men denied apotheosis,
bankrupt, on horseback, welded to their horses,
    moved
white marble rearing moon-shaped hooves,
to strike the country down.

Romantic military sculpture
waved sabers over Dickensian architecture,
laconic squads patrolled the blanks
left by the invisible poor.

All day I read about newspaper coup d'états
of the leaden, internecine generals—
lumps of dough on the chessboard—and never saw
their countermarching tanks.

Along the sunlit cypress walks
of the Republican Martyrs' graveyard,
hundreds of one-room Roman temples
hugged their neo-classical catafalques.

Literal commemorative busts
preserved the frogged coats
and fussy, furrowed foreheads
of those soldier bureaucrats.

By their brazen doors
a hundred marble goddesses
wept like willows. I found rest
by cupping a soft palm to each hard breast.

That night I walked the streets.
My pinched feet bled in my shoes. In a park
I fought off seduction from the dark
python bodies of new world demigods.

Everywhere, the bellowing of the old bull—
the muzzled underdogs still roared
for the brute beef of Peron,
the nymphets' Don Giovanni.

On the main square
a white stone obelisk
rose like a phallus
without flesh or hair—

always my lighthouse homeward to the hotel!
My breath whitened the winter air,
I was the worse for wear.

When the night's blackness spilled,
I saw the light of morning
on Buenos Aires filled
with frowning, starch-collared crowds.

Déjeuner sur l'Herbe

by Mary McCarthy

"You can cut into *The Naked Lunch* at any intersection point," says Burroughs, suiting the action to the word, in "an atrophied preface" he appends as a tail-piece. His book, he means, is like a neighborhood movie with continuous showings that you can drop into whenever you please—you don't have to wait for the beginning of the feature picture. Or like a worm that you can chop up into sections each of which wriggles off as an independent worm. Or a nine-lived cat. Or a cancer. He is fond of the word "mosaic," especially in its scientific sense of a plant-mottling caused by a virus, and his Muse (see etymology of "mosaic") is interested in organic processes of multiplication and duplication. The literary notion of time as simultaneous, a montage, is not original with Burroughs; what is original is the scientific bent he gives it and a view of the world that combines biochemistry, anthropology, and politics. It is as though *Finnegans Wake* were cut loose from history and adapted for a cinerama circus titled "One World." *The Naked Lunch* has no use for history, which is all "ancient history"—sloughed-off skin; from its planetary perspective, there are only geography and customs. Seen in terms of space, history shrivels into a mere wrinkling or furrowing of the surface as in an aerial relief-map or one of those pieced-together aerial photographs known in the trade as mosaics. The oldest memory in *The Naked Lunch* is of jacking-off in boyhood latrines, a memory recaptured through pederasty. This must be

the first space novel, the first serious piece of science fiction—
the others are entertainment.

The action of *The Naked Lunch* takes place in the consciousness of One Man, William Lee, who is taking a drug
cure. The principal characters, besides Lee, are his friend, Bill
Gains (who seems momentarily to turn into a woman called
Jane), various members of the Narcotic Squad, especially one
Bradley the Buyer, Dr. Benway, a charlatan medico who is
treating Lee, two vaudevillians, Clem and Jody, A. J., a carnival
con man, the last of the Big Spenders, a sailor, an Arab called
Ahmed, an archetypal Southern druggist, Doc Parker ("a
man don't have no secrets from God and his druggist"), and
various boys with whining voices. Among the minor characters
are a number of automobiles, each with its specific complaint, like the oil-burning Ford V-8, a film executive, the Party
Leader, the Vigilante, John and Mary, the sex acrobats, and a
puzzled American housewife who is heard complaining because the Mixmaster keeps trying to climb up under her dress.
The scene shifts about, shiftily, from New York to Chicago
to St. Louis to New Orleans to Mexico to Malmo, Sweden,
Venice, and the human identities shift about shiftily too, for all
these modern places and modern individuals (if that is the
right word) have interchangeable parts. Burroughs is fond too
of the word "ectoplasm," and the beings that surround Lee,
particularly the inimical ones, seem ectoplasmic phantoms
projected on the wide screen of his consciousness from a mass
seance. But the haunting is less visual than auditory. These
"characters," in the colloquial sense, are ventriloquial voices
produced, as it were, against the will of the ventriloquist, who
has become their dummy. Passages of dialogue and description keep recurring in different contexts with slight variations,
as though they possessed ubiquity.

The best comparison for the book, with its aerial sex acts
performed on a high trapeze, its con men and barkers, its

arena-like form, is in fact a circus. A circus travels but it is always the same, and this is Burroughs' sardonic image of modern life. The Barnum of the show is the mass-manipulator, who appears in a series of disguises. *Control*, as Burroughs says, underlining it, *can never be a means to anything but more control—like drug*s, and the vicious circle of addiction is reenacted, worldwide, with sideshows in the political and "social" sphere—the social here has vanished, except in quotation marks, like the historical, for everything has become automatized. Everyone is an addict of one kind or another, as people indeed are wont to say of themselves, complacently: "I'm a crossword puzzle addict, a High-Fi addict," etcetera. The South is addicted to lynching and nigger-hating, and the Southern folk-custom of burning a Negro recurs throughout the book as a sort of Fourth-of-July carnival with fireworks. Circuses, with their cages of wild animals, are also dangerous, like Burroughs's human circus; an accident may occur, as when the electronic brain in Dr. Benway's laboratory goes on the rampage, and the freaks escape to mingle with the controlled citizens of Freeland in a general riot, or in the scene where the hogs are let loose in the gourmet restaurant.

On a level usually thought to be "harmless," addiction to platitudes and commonplaces is global. To Burroughs's ear, the Bore, lurking in the hotel lobby; is literally deadly ("'You look to me like a man of intelligence.' Always ominous opening words, my boy!"). The same for Doc Parker with his captive customer in the back room of his pharmacy ("…so long as you got a legitimate condition and an Rx from a certified bona feedy M.D., I'm honored to serve you"), the professor in the classroom ("Hehe hehe he"), the attorney in court ("Hehe hehe he," likewise). The complacent sound of snickering laughter is an alarm signal, like the suave bell-tones of the psychiatrist and the emphatic drone of the Party Leader ("You see men and women. *Ordinary* men and women going about their ordinary everyday tasks. Leading their ordinary lives. That's what we need...").

Cut to ordinary men and women, going about their ordinary everyday tasks. The whine of the put-upon boy hustler: "All kinda awful sex acts." "Why cancha just get physical like a human?" "So I guess he come to some kinda awful climax." "You think I am innarested to hear about your horrible old condition? I am not innarested at all." "But he comes to a climax and turns into some kinda awful crab." This aggrieved tone merges with the malingering sighs of the American housewife, opening a box of Lux: "I got the most awful cold, and my intestines is all constipated." And the clarion of the Salesman: "When the Priority numbers are called up yonder I'll be there." These average folks are addicts of the science page of the Sunday supplements; they like to talk about their diseases and about vile practices that paralyze the practitioner from the waist down or about a worm that gets into your kidney and grows to enormous size or about the "horrible" result of marijuana addiction—it makes you turn black and your legs drop off. The superstitious scientific vocabulary is diffused from the laboratory and the mental hospital into the general population. Overheard at a lynching: "Don't crowd too close, boys. His intestines is subject to explode in the fire." The same diffusion of culture takes place with modern physics. A lieutenant to his general: "But, chief, can't we get them started and they imitate each other like a chained reaction?"

The phenomenon of repetition, of course, gives rise to boredom; many readers complain that they cannot get through *The Naked Lunch*. And/or that they find it disgusting. It *is* disgusting and sometimes tiresome, often in the same places. The prominence of the anus, of feces, and of all sorts of "horrible" discharges, as the characters would say, from the body's orifices, becomes too much of a bad thing, like the sadomasochistic sex performances—the automatic ejaculation of a hanged man is not everybody's cantharides. A reader whose erogenous zones are more temperate than the author's begins to feel either that he is a square (a guilty sentiment he should not yield to) or that he is the captive of an addict.

In defense, Swift could be cited, and indeed between Burroughs and Swift there are many points of comparison; not only the obsession with excrement and the horror of female genitalia but a disgust with politics and the whole body politic. Like Swift, Burroughs has irritable nerves and something of the crafty temperament of the inventor. There is a great deal of Laputa in the countries Burroughs calls Interzone and Freeland, and Swift's solution for the Irish problem would appeal to the American's dry logic. As Gulliver, Swift posed as an anthropologist (though the study was not known by that name then) among savage people; Burroughs parodies the anthropologist in his descriptions of the American heartland: "...the Interior a vast subdivision, antennae of television to the meaningless sky.... Illinois and Missouri, miasma of mound building peoples, grovelling worship of the Food Source, cruel and ugly festivals." The style here is more emotive than Swift's, but in his deadpan explanatory notes ("This is a rural English custom designed to eliminate aged and bedfast dependents") there is a Swiftian factuality. The "factual" appearance of the whole narrative, with its battery of notes and citations, some straight, some loaded, its extracts from a diary, like a ship's log, its pharmacopeia, has the flavor of eighteenth-century satire. He calls himself a "Factualist" and belongs, all alone, to an Age of Reason, which he locates in the future. In him, as in Swift, there is a kind of soured utopianism.

Yet what saves *The Naked Lunch* is not a literary ancestor but humor. Burroughs's humor is peculiarly American, at once broad and sly. It is the humor of a comedian, a vaudeville performer playing in *One*, in front of the asbestos curtain to some

Keith Circuit or Pantages house long since converted to
movies. The same jokes reappear, slightly refurbished, to suit
the circumstances, the way a vaudeville artist used to change
Yonkers to Renton when he was playing Seattle. For example,
the Saniflush joke, which is always good for a laugh: somebody
is cutting the cocaine/the morphine/the penicillin with
Saniflush. Some of the jokes are verbal ("Stop me if you've
heard this atomic secret" or Dr. Benway's "A simopath...is a
citizen convinced he is an ape or other simian. It is a disorder
peculiar to the army and discharge cures it"). Some are mimic
buffoonery (Dr. Benway, in his last appearance, dreamily, his
voice fading out: "Cancer, my first love"). Some are whole
vaudeville "numbers," as when the hoofers, Clem and Jody, are
hired by the Russians to give Americans a bad name abroad:
they appear in Liberia wearing black Stetsons and red galluses
and talking loudly about burning niggers back home. A skit
like this may rise to a frenzy, as if in a Marx Brothers or a
Clayton, Jackson, and Durante act. *E.g.*, the very funny scene
in Chez Robert, "where a huge icy gourmet broods over the
greatest cuisine in the world": A. J. appears, the last of the Big
Spenders, and orders a bottle of ketchup; immediate pandemonium; A. J. gives his hog-call, and the shocked gourmet din-
ers are all devoured by famished hogs. The effect of
pandemonium, all hell breaking loose, is one of Burroughs's
favorites and an equivalent of the old vaudeville finale, with
the acrobats, the jugglers, the magician, the hoofers, the lady-
who-was-cut-in-half, the piano player, the comedians, all push-
ing into the act.

Another favorite effect, with Burroughs, is the metamorphosis. A citizen is turned into animal form, a crab or a huge
centipede, or into some unspeakable monstrosity like Bradley
the Narcotics Agent who turns into an unidentifiable carnivore. These metamorphoses, of course, are punishments. The
Hellzapoppin effect of orgies and riots and the metamorpho-

sis effect, rapid or creeping, are really cancerous onslaughts—matter on the rampage multiplying itself and "building" as a revue scene "builds" to a climax. Growth and deterioration are the same thing: a human being "deteriorates" or "grows" into a one-man jungle. What you think of it depends on your point of view; from the junkie's angle, Bradley is better as a carnivore eating the Narcotics Commissioner than he was as "fuzz"— junky slang for the police.

The impression left by this is perplexing. On the one hand, control is evil; on the other, escape from control is mass slaughter or reduction to a state of proliferating cellular matter. The police are the enemy, but as Burroughs shrewdly observes in one passage: "A *functioning* police state needs no police." The policeman is internalized in the citizen. You might say that it would have been better to have no control, no police, in the first place; then there would be no police states, functioning or otherwise. This would seem to be Burroughs's position, but it is not consistent with his picture of sex. The libertarian position usually has as one of its axioms a love of Nature and the natural, that is, of the life-principle itself, commonly identified with sex. But there is little overt love of the life-principle in *The Naked Lunch*, and sex, while magnified— a common trait of homosexual literature—is a kind of mechanical mantrap baited with fresh meat. The sexual climax, the jet of sperm, accompanied by a whistling scream, is often a death spasm, and the "perfect" orgasm would seem to be the posthumous orgasm of the hanged man, shooting his jissom into pure space.

It is true that Nature and sex are two-faced and that growth is death-oriented. But if Nature is not seen as far more good than evil, then a need for control is posited. And, strangely, this seems to be Burroughs's position too. *The human virus can now be treated*, he says with emphasis, meaning the species itself. By scientific methods, he implies. Yet the laboratory of *The Naked Lunch* is a musical-comedy inferno, and Dr. Benway's assistant is a female chimpanzee. It is impossible, as Burroughs knows, to have scientific experiment without control. Then what? Self-control? Do-it-yourself? But self-control, again, is an internalized system of authority, a subjection of the impulse to the will, the least "natural" part of the personality. Such a system might suit Marcus Aurelius, but it hardly seems congenial to the author of *The Naked Lunch*. And even if it were (for the author is at once puritan and tolerant), it would not form the basis for scientific experiment on the "human virus." Only for scientific experiment on oneself.

Possibly this is what Burroughs means: in fact his present literary exercises may be stages in such a deliberate experiment. The questions just posed would not arise if *The Naked Lunch* did not contain messages that unluckily are somewhat arcane. Not just messages; prescriptions. That—to answer a pained question that keeps coming up like a refrain—is why the book is taken seriously. Burroughs's remarkable talent is only part of the reason; the other part is that, finally, for the first time in recent years, a talented writer means what he says to be taken and used literally, like an Rx prescription. The literalness of Burroughs is the opposite of "literature." Unsentimental and factual, he writes as though his thoughts had the quality of self-evidence. In short, he has a crankish courage, but all courage nowadays is probably crankish.

Grub Street: New York

by Elizabeth Hardwick

Making a living is nothing; the great difficulty is making a point, making a difference—with words. Here in New York you walk about the shattered, but still unreformed, streets and it seems the city has suffered a scar or wound that has not only changed its appearance but altered its purpose and deepest nature. Outside my house the old Central Park Stables are empty, the windows broken. The warm yellow brick and faded blue trim still glow in the afternoon sun; pigeons tend their nests inside, squatting until the verdict is handed down about this waiting, hurt space. One does not know what to reject, what old alley of desolation to resent, what corner of newness to despise. If one hardly knows what to reject, how much harder it is to be oneself rejected. Is there anyone who hasn't, as we say in our expressive rhetoric, *made it*?

Yes, some old grubbers, still suffering. The door bell rings and you are face to face with an outcast who has come on some errand of career that can never be accomplished. He is dark, rather small and thin, hostile and yet briefly hopeful, brightly beaming with suspiciousness. A relief to believe his desperation and obsolescence are somehow closer to litera-ture than to life. He seems to be out of a novel rather than to be writing a novel. Good! True characters, men with a classical twitch, are still alive, old veterans with their frayed flags, crea-tures such as fiction used to tell of. But the man is not a charac-ter in a book; he is himself a writer. His theme is, "If you're not a pederast, a junkie, a Negro—not even a 'white Negro,' ha, ha!—you haven't a dog's chance! Just put your foot in a publisher's office and someone will step on it!" This novelist, in his middle fifties, has known a regular recurrence of literary disaster; and yet he has stayed on the old homestead, planting seeds year after year, like those farmers in drought places who greet each season's dryness with anguished surprise. Even teaching, our first and last refuge, had closed its heart after the poor writer gave out too many failing grades. With his special beam of despairing self-satisfaction, he said, "The students know no more about punctuation than a fly in the air! No, I will not have an illiterate Ph.D. on my conscience." Unpleasant, insignificant, intransigent man—born without an accommodating joint, trying to grasp without thumbs. But, indeed, he makes his point; a certain pleasure, or relief, lies in the assurance that a genuine paranoid solidity cannot be absorbed by American life, that it will not break to the crush of the tooth. And that is a sort of role, perhaps.

Age and outmoded purity and patience may kill sometimes. Old lady writers, without means, without Social Security, reading in bed all day—dear old Sibyls, almost forgotten, hardly called upon except perhaps at midnight by a drunken couple from a pad down the street. Failure is not funny. It is cockroaches on the service elevator, old men in carpet slippers waiting anxiously by the mail slots in the lobby, neighborhood walks where the shops, graphs of consumption, show only a clutter of broken vases, strings of cracked beads, dirty feathers, an old vaudevillian's memorable dinner jacket and decades of cast-off books—the dust of ambition from which the eye turns away in misery.

But the young, the active, rely upon themselves, or perhaps they are desperately thrown back upon themselves, literally. The drama of real life will not let down the prose writer. He can camp for a while in the sedgy valley of autobiography, of current happenings, of the exploration of his own sufferings and sensations, the record of people met, of national figures contemplated. There is beauty to be torn out of the event, the suicide, the murder case, the prize fight. The "I," undisguised, visits new regions for us and pours all his art into them. Life inspires. The confession, the revelation, are not reporting, nor even journalism. Real life is presented *as if it were* fiction. The concreteness of fact is made suggestive, shadowy, symbolical. The vividly experiencing "I" begins his search for his art in the newspapers.

From the first the reader is captivated by his surprise that this particular writer should be a witness to this particular event. We are immediately engaged by a biographical incongruity: Dwight Macdonald, the famous radical, with his beard, his "ideas" on Doris Day; Norman Mailer on Sonny Liston; William Styron on a poor convict up for parole; the novelist John Phillips on Teddy Kennedy's campaign. Truman Capote is writing an entire book on an interesting murder case in Kansas and is even said to have provided the police with an important clue. Capote left his villa in Switzerland and went to the bereft, gritty little town in Kansas to study the drama of the trial. An author's unexpected marriage to his subject is in many ways the essence of each new plot.

Real events, one's own vices completely understood, will have a certain, and sometimes, a pure interest. It *works*, it is *convincing*. Actuality sustains in a world that does not appear to care very much for fiction writing. In art, the labels from a can of soup, the design of motor cars, the square of the American flag—objects from everyday life put on to canvas— announce themselves as a protest against the idealism and tyranny of abstract expressionism. Imaginary people, fabricated loves and deaths, conclusions not given but to be created in loneliness: Are these not also a tyranny from which the writer will some day shrink? Another puzzle: much good writing appears in entertainment magazines other writers seldom read. Circulation without audience. The re-creation of what has truly happened is a self-propelled activity, addressed to no one in particular. Or should we accept the need for money? "What God abandoned, these defended, and saved the sum of things for pay."

Art as a religion—Rilke—seems to be passing; not the work of Rilke, but the style of life, the austere dedication, sustained by the hope that poems and novels would save us. Those holy pages, produced in pain (Flaubert: "You don't know what it is to stay a whole day with your head in your hands trying to squeeze your unfortunate brain so as to find a word")—is there time? From patience, at last, they had perfection. And a security, a fringe benefit, a pension fund such as one can hardly imagine nowadays. Think! Richard Ellmann tells us that Joyce thought the worst thing about World War II was that it distracted the world from reading *Finnegans Wake*.

Glass is the perfect material of our life. James Baldwin recently had a long, astonishing essay in *The New Yorker*. The work began as an unbearable memoir of Baldwin's youth in Harlem, but it did not remain simply a painful memoir. It became one of those "children in the hands of an angry God" sermons on the Hell of American life for the Negro. Baldwin was determined to make us feel each unutterable day of suffering and humiliation, to make us cringe from the fraud of the democracy and Christianity that had betrayed the Negroes, those most faithful in their devotions. The work was written in a mood of desperation, with full eloquence and intellectual force—and with something more. It was clearly threatening. Baldwin felt the Negro to be approaching a final, revengeful fury.

So there it was. Everyone read it. Everyone talked about it and seemed to feel in some way the better for it. The guerrilla warfare by which the weak become strong, or at least destructive—even the threat of that could be taken, apparently, accepted, turned into glass. Only Russia and communism arouse—there, writer, watch out.

A peculiar glut, historically interesting. But who wants to be a cook in a household of obese people? The poor, the hungry, fly in by air, brought on official visits, missions of culture. A South American in a brushed, blue serge suit, wearing polished black shoes and large cufflinks of semiprecious stones. His fingernails and his careful, neat dress tell you of all the polish, the care, the melancholy mending done at home by mothers and sisters. This man was one of those whom struggle had drained dry. He had arrived, by hideously hard work, at an overwhelming pedantry, a bachelorish violence of self-control. The pedantry of scarcity. This pale glacier had been produced in the tropics, a poor man in a poor country, trying to lift himself into the professions, to cut through the jungle of deprivation, save a few pennies of ambition from the national bankruptcy. At last with his nervous precision, his aching repression, he declared that the huge, romantic, excessive Thomas Wolfe was the American with whom he felt the closest spiritual and personal connection. He meant to write a book on Wolfe, in Portuguese. He sat looking out of the window, glumly taking in the commercial spires in the distance; his sallow, yearning spirit seemed to have come forth from some mute backland in which his efforts had a bitter, pioneer necessity. Thomas Wolfe! He blinked. "He is my life."

At the entrance to the subway station, there is often an archaic figure giving out a folded sheet of information about the Socialist Labor Party, or some other small, oddly extant group. In only a few minutes after the distributor takes up his post the streets are littered with his offering. The pages are not thrown away in resentment or disagreement, but cast down as if they were bits of Kleenex: clean white paper with nothing at all written on it, falling into the gutter.

Adam as a Welshman

by W. H. Auden

Anathemata might be described as an epic about the two Adams. Perhaps it may help the reader to approach what is, frankly, a very difficult poem, if he will imagine, as he reads it, that he is sitting in a Roman Catholic church while Mass is being celebrated. What is going on at the altar starts a train of thoughts and memories, his mind goes wool-gathering, and he forgets where he is, until some sound or sight recalls him to a consciousness of where he is; this in its turn starts a new train of thought, and so on. What the priest is doing in the middle of the twentieth century—he does it every day in exactly the same manner, and for many centuries it has always and everywhere been repeated thus—he does in anamnesis of something which only happened once, and will never happen again.

> During the reign of the Emperor
> *Tiberius Claudius Nero Caesar*
>
> > *voted the tribune's powers for the*
> *first time twenty-five years since; his fourth term consul*
> *nine years gone.*
> > In Jerusalem
> *Under the fifth procurator*
> > *of Judaea*
> *in the third or fourth*
> > *severe*

> April
>
> *of the ten, sharp*
>
> > *Aprils of his office.*
>
> *On Ariel mountain*

The "creatures" of the rite are bread and wine, the existence of which presupposes both a nonhuman nature which produces wheat and grapes, and a human culture which by thought and labor is able to convert these natural products into human artifacts. With these symbolic signs he reenacts or represents the sacrifice on the cross of Christ, the Second Adam, for the redemption of the first Adam, that is to say, all mankind, whether dead, living, or unborn. As a person who can say "I," every human being, however he may be classifiable biologically and culturally, is unique—no one like him has ever existed before or will again—and, in consequence, every human being is Adam, an incarnation of all mankind. This unique "I" can never be the topic of speech; we can only communicate with each other *about* objects and events of this or that class. Yet, whenever a man's speech is authentic, the way in which he speaks of such objects and events is uniquely his so that, in order to understand him, we have to translate what he says into our own unique speech, which, like his, consists, one might say, exclusively of Proper Nouns.

The difficulty of such translation which is implicit in all personal communication, above all in poetry, is manifest in *Anathemata* in an unusually severe way. It would be interesting to make a critical comparison of Mr. David Jones and M. St. John Perse, whose poems are also epics about the First Adam (though not about the Second). If, and this is a big If, the reader has an absolute command of the French language, M. St. John Perse's poetry seems much easier to grasp because it contains no Proper Nouns. Particularity and concreteness are there in plenty, but it is largely a particularity of action and function; one thinks of the long catalogs of curious human occupations, prefaced by the rubric "he who." But these human actions do not occur in any particular place or time; in M. St. John Perse's poetic universe there are neither calendars nor atlases. In Mr. Jones's poetic universe, on the other hand, Proper Nouns (all foreign words partake of the nature of Proper Nouns), calendars, and atlases are the most conspicuous features, and one must admit that without the copious notes which Mr. Jones provides, it is unlikely that *anyone* except the author would be able fully to understand the poem. I myself have read it many times since it first appeared ten years ago and there are still many passages which I do not "get." In his defense, however, one must point out that M. St. John Perse's picture of humanity is necessarily, by its timelessness and placelessness, lacking in a sense of human motive and purpose; his Adam has no history, and it is Adam's history in which Mr. Jones is most interested.

The Adam of *Anathemata* is a man old enough to have fought in the First World War, a Catholic convert, interested in the arts (Mr. Jones is a painter as well as a writer), archaeology, mythology, and liturgics, to whom as a child Malory and the Mabinogian obviously meant much, and on whose writing the most clearly distinguished influence has been James Joyce. The self he has inherited from his parents and ancestors is a member of a number of concentric and overlapping classes, to each of which the various sections of his poem are, roughly speaking, dedicated.

Thus the opening section, "Rite and Fore-Time," is mainly concerned with himself as a member of the human species, Earth's "adaptable, rational, elect and plucked-out otherling" who probably first appeared during the Tertiary Period:

Before the drift
               was over the lime-face.
Sometime between the final and the penultimate débâcle.
               (Already Arcturus deploys his reconnoitering
chills in greater strength: soon his last Putsch *on any scale.)*
Before this all but proto-historic transmogrification of the
land-face.
Just before they rigged the half-lit stage for dim-eyed Clio
to step with some small confidence the measures of her
brief and lachrymal pavan.

and can be distinguished from his nearest co-laterals by certain characteristics such as speech, the use of tools, and sacred
cults.

    "Middle-Sea and Lear-sea" is concerned with himself as a
Western European who is what he is because of certain historical events peculiar to Western Europe, such as the civilization
of Crete and the Doric Invasions,

One thousand two hundred years
               since the Dorian jarls
rolled up the map of Arcady and the transmontane storm-
groups fractured the archaic pattern…
               From the tomb of the strife-years the
new-born shapes begin already to look uncommonly like the
brats of mother Europa.
We begin already to discern our own.
Are the proto-forms already ours?
Is that the West-wind on our cheek-bones?

But it's early—very grey and early in our morning and most
irradiance is yet reflected from far-side Our sea, the Nile
moon still shines on the Hittite creatures and Crete still
shows the Argives how.

and, of course, the establishment of the Roman Empire, which brought the whole Mediterranean area under one rule.

...at the intersected place he caused our sacred commerce to be. Why yes—west he took himself off, on the base-line he traced and named when he traced it: decumanus. *West-turn from his* kardo *I saw him go, over his right* transversus. *From to rear of him I discerned his marcher's lurch—I'd breath to see that.*
West-star, hers and all!
brighting the hooped turn of his scapular-plates enough to show his pelvic sway and the hunch of his robber's shoulders. Though he was of the Clarissimi his aquila over me was robbery
'T's a great robbery
—is empire.

Then he is an inhabitant of the British Isles and a Londoner of Welsh stock whose culture and language would not be what they are but for the peculiar history of Britain which was not Romanized until after the beginning of the Christian era and then never completely, and where the original Celtic population was driven into the Welsh mountains or submerged under successive waves of Teutonic invaders, the Saxons, the Vikings, the Normans.

From the fora
                to the forests.
Out from gens Romulum
        into the Weal-*kin*
dinas-*man gone* aethwlad
cives *gone wold-men*
                ...from Lindum to London
bridges broken down.

There is a great deal of imagery in the poem derived from ships and seafaring. It was seafaring merchants in search of tin who first brought the remote island of Britain to the attention of the civilized Mediterranean. Britain was destined to become a great maritime power and London one of the great ports of the world. It is only natural, therefore, that such a seafaring people should use nautical imagery as symbols for the historical adventure of mankind. As Mr. Jones says in one of his notes:

> What is pleaded in the Mass is precisely the argosy or voyage of the Redeemer, consisting of his entire sufferings and his death, his conquest of Hades, his resurrection and his return in triumph to heaven. It is this that is offered to the Trinity on behalf of us argonauts and of the whole argosy of mankind, and, in some sense, of all sentient being, and, perhaps, of insentient too.

Of the communication problems which this kind of poetry presents, Mr. Jones is very well aware and he has stated them in his preface much better than I could.

> The poet may feel something with regard to Penda the Mercian and nothing with regard to Darius the Mede. In itself that is a limitation, it might be regarded as a disproportion; no matter, there is no help—he must work within the limits of his love. There must be no mugging-up, no "ought to know" or "try to feel"; for only what is actually loved and known can be seen *sub specie aeternitatis*. The nurse herself is adamant about this: she is indifferent to what the poet may wish to feel, she cares only for what he in fact feels.

> The words "May they rest in peace" and the words "Whosoever will" might by some feat of artistry, be so juxtaposed within a context as not only to translate the

words "*Requiescat in pace*" and "*Quicunque vult*," but to evoke the *exact historic over-tones and under-tones* of those Latin words. But should some writer find himself unable by whatever ingenuity of formal arrangement or of contextual allusion to achieve this identity of content and identity of evocation, while changing the language, then he would have no alternative but to use the original form.... It is not a question of "translation" or even of "finding an equivalent word"; it is something much more complex. "Tsar" will mean one thing and "Caesar" another to the end of time.

The artist deals wholly in signs. His signs must be valid, that is, valid for him and, normally, for the culture that has made him. But there is a time factor affecting these signs. If a requisite now-ness is not present, the sign, valid in itself, is apt to suffer a kind of invalidation. This presents most complicated problems to the artist working outside a reasonably static culture-phase.... It may be that the kind of thing I have been trying to make is no longer makeable in the kind of way in which I have tried to make it.

It is certainly true that no reader is going to be able to make Mr. Jones's "now-ness" his own without taking a great deal of trouble and many rereadings of *Anathemata*, and, if he says: "I'm sorry, Mr. Jones is asking too much. I have neither the time nor the patience which he seems to expect me to bring to his poem," I do not know what argument one could use to convince him otherwise. I can only state my personal experience, namely, that I have found the time and trouble I have taken with *Anathemata* infinitely rewarding.

Punching Papa

by Norman Mailer

There is an irony which usually defeats the memoir and makes it an inferior art. The man who can tell a good story in company about his friends is usually not able to find a prose which can capture the nuances of his voice. Invariably, the language is leached out—the account tends to have a droning episodic quality as if some movie queen were recounting the separate toils of her lovers to a tape recorder.

Now the worst to be said for *That Summer in Paris* is that Morley Callaghan has not altogether avoided this blight. Using himself as a character of reasonable dimensions, an honest sensible hard-nosed ego-bastard, a talented short story writer, a good husband, a good Irish-Catholic, a good college boxer, and a good expatriate, his memoir is built on the premise that catgut is good for stringing pearls. So one is taken by Callaghan for a three-to-five page description of each of his separate meetings with Maxwell Perkins, Sherwood Anderson, Ford Madox Ford, Josephine Herbst, Sinclair Lewis, Robert McAlmon, Sylvia Beach, James Joyce, Pauline Hemingway, Michael Arlen, Ludwig Lewisohn, Allen Tate, Edward Titus, Joan Miró, and Zelda Fitzgerald. It is dim writing. One has only to compare the chapter he gives to Sinclair Lewis (one of the more elaborate cameos) against some equivalent number of pages Wolfe devoted to a similar portrait, and the result is no contest. A deadness comes back from Callaghan's echo. His short portraits are written at the level of a conversation with somebody who might tell you he met Truman Capote.

"Well," you might respond, "what is he like?"

"Well," says your friend, "he's small, you know, and he's kind of bright."

If one knows some of the people mentioned, or is obsessed with the period, then Morley Callaghan's memoir will satisfy. But it is not a good book. It is in fact a modest bad dull book which contains a superb short story about Hemingway, Fitzgerald, and Callaghan. One can push so far as to say it is probably the most dramatic single story about Hemingway's relation to Fitzgerald in the literature. If Callaghan had been ready to stop at this, he could have had a long short story or a short memoir which might have become a classic. Instead he attenuated his material over a run of 255 pages, and so reminds one of a remark Fitzgerald once made to Callaghan. Talking about *The Great Gatsby*, he said the book had done reasonably well but was hardly a best seller. "It was too short a book," Fitzgerald said. "Remember this, Morley. Never write a book under sixty thousand words."

That's it. Callaghan has remembered, and has proceeded to stretch it out. As literature, it's a mistake. Financially, Fitzgerald's advice might still prove wise. The author now has a book instead of a story; the value of a movie sale is increased. The story about Hemingway, Fitzgerald, and Callaghan done by John Huston, produced by Sam Spiegel, could make a very good movie. For the first time one has the confidence that an eyewitness has been able to cut a bona fide trail through the charm, the mystery, and the curious perversity of Hemingway's personality. One gets a good intimation of what was very bad in the man, and the portrait is reinforced by the fact that Callaghan was not out to damage the reputation—on the contrary, he is nearly obsessed by the presence of taint in a man he considers great.

In turn, Fitzgerald is also admired. In fact he is even loved as a friend, loved perhaps more than Hemingway. Yet Callaghan fixes his character for our attention. Like many an American writer to come after him, Fitzgerald was one of those men who do not give up early on the search to acquire more manhood for themselves. His method was to admire men who were strong. In this sense he was a salesman. When the beloved object did not smile back, Fitzgerald, like Willy Loman, looked into an earthquake. We are offered Fitzgerald at just such a moment.

Talking to Callaghan one day, Fitzgerald referred to Hemingway's ability as a boxer, and remarked that while Hemingway was probably not good enough to be heavyweight champion of the world, he was undoubtedly as good as Young Stribling, the light-heavyweight champion. "Look, Scott," said Callaghan, "Ernest is an amateur. I'm an amateur. All this talk is ridiculous." Unconvinced, Fitzgerald asked to come along to the gym at the American Club and watch Hemingway and Callaghan box. But Callaghan has let the reader in earlier on one small point. Hemingway, four inches taller and forty pounds heavier than Callaghan, "may have thought about boxing, dreamed about it, consorted with old fighters and hung around gyms," but Callaghan "had done more actual boxing with men who could box a little and weren't just taking exercise or fooling around."

So on an historic afternoon in June in Paris in 1929, Hemingway and Callaghan boxed a few rounds with Fitzgerald serving as timekeeper. The second round went on for a long time. Both men began to get tired, Hemingway got careless. Callaghan caught him a good punch and dropped Hemingway on his back. At the next instant Fitzgerald cried out, "Oh, my God! I let the round go four minutes."

"All right, Scott," Ernest said. "If you want to see me getting the shit knocked out of me, just say so. Only don't say you made a mistake."

According to Callaghan's estimate, Scott never recovered from that moment. One believes it. Four months later, a cruel and wildly inaccurate story about this episode appeared in the *Herald Tribune* book section. It was followed by a cable sent collect by Fitzgerald at Hemingway's insistence. "HAVE SEEN STORY IN HERALD TRIBUNE. ERNEST AND I AWAIT YOUR CORRECTION. SCOTT FITZGERALD."

Since Callaghan had already written such a letter to the paper, none of the three men could ever forgive each other.

As the vignettes, the memoirs, and the biographies of Hemingway proliferate, Callaghan's summer in Paris may take on an importance beyond its literary merit, for it offers a fine clue to the logic of Hemingway's mind, and tempts one to make the prediction that there will be no definitive biography of Hemingway until the nature of his personal torture is better comprehended. It is possible Hemingway lived every day of his life in the style of the suicide. What a great dread is that. It is the dread which sits in the silences of his short declarative sentences. At any instant, by any failure in magic, by a mean defeat, or by a moment of cowardice, Hemingway could be thrust back again into the agonizing demands of his courage. For the life of his talent must have depended on living in a psychic terrain where one must either be brave beyond one's limit, or sicken closer into a bad illness, or, indeed, by the ultimate logic of the suicide, must advance the hour in which one would make another reconnaissance into one's death.

That may be why Hemingway turned in such fury on Fitzgerald. To be knocked down by a smaller man could only imprison him further into the dread he was forever trying to avoid. Each time his physical vanity suffered a defeat, he would be forced to embark on a new existential gamble with his life. So he would naturally think of Fitzgerald's little error as an act of treachery, for the result of that extra minute in the second round could only be a new bout of anxiety which would drive his instinct into ever more dangerous situations. Most men find their profoundest passion in looking for a way toescape their private and secret torture. It is not likely that Hemingway was a brave man who sought danger for the sake of the sensations it provided him. What is more likely the truth of his long odyssey is that he struggled with his cowardice and against a secret lust to suicide all of his life, that his inner landscape was a nightmare, and he spent his nights wrestling with the gods. It may even be that the final judgment on his work may come to the notion that what he failed to do was tragic, but what he accomplished was heroic, for it is possible he carried a weight of anxiety within him from day to day which would have suffocated any man smaller than himself. There are two kinds of brave men. Those who are brave by the grace of nature, and those who are brave by an act of will. It is the merit of Callaghan's long anecdote that the second condition is suggested to be Hemingway's own.

Auden's Prose

by John Berryman

Since many readers will be as pleased as this reviewer that Auden has put together a fat selection of his critical writings of recent years, and since it goes without saying that Auden's opinions are important because they are his, I want to look into the curious fact that he does not really sound like a professional critic and perhaps is not one.

Perhaps he is too modest and too generous. These virtues shine again and again from these pages, and they are remarkable enough in one of the chief poets of the age, a man internationally celebrated now for thirty years, also a man known in his legend for a witty, savaging tongue, whereas here he several times refuses to exemplify a Bad Work on the ground that to do so would be "cruel." But probably a critic must take the moral risk and be tougher, for it is his job, among other things, to assert and to judge: to propagate the faith and only the faith.

Worse still, he writes too well. His critical prose is not up to William Empson's or Edmund Wilson's, being even more informal than the one and less cunningly organized than the other; but that these names come up is tribute enough. (His imaginative prose, in *The Orators*, is brilliant.) He sounds like a man talking it out, while some very able modern critics sound like computers, or wasps, or mediums.

Then we have his engaging admission in the foreword that "I have never written a line of criticism except in response to a demand by others for a lecture, an introduction, a review, etc.;

though I hope that some love went into their writing, I wrote them because I needed the money." In short, he has no Program. He is not selling anything. Now a proper critic is as zealous as a young poet, crawling with ideas he burns to spread and enforce. (It is odd, by the way, that a poet so theoretical and programmatic as Auden—few poets in any time have created a whole moral landscape, as he did in the Thirties—should go laissez-faire in his criticism.)

Finally, there is his reviewing practice. It is hardly unfair to say that Auden, over the years, has done one of two things with books entrusted to him for comment: either he wrote about what interested him at the moment, making some spidery connection with the book in hand, or, with books he felt keen about, like Cyril Connolly's vivid *Enemies of Promise*, he quoted from them at agreeable length. Surely the pro sits on and breaks his brains.

So maybe Auden is not a professional critic. Splendid. He is a professional writer, of course, but in this corner an amateur—in the good sense of that sad word. He loves. He reports his love. Once, in a piece on Thomas Hardy not here reprinted (it was in *The Southern Review*), he observed that he was in love with Hardy. So are we all; but who else has said so?

The showpiece of the book is a study of the Master-Servant relation in literature, "Balaam and his Ass": Quixote-Sancho, Lear-Fool, Giovanni-Leporello, others. For illustration of his interests and power, the opening sentence and a remark about *The Tempest* will do. "The relation between Master and Servant is not given by nature or fate but comes into being through an act of conscious volition." "*The Tempest* seems to me a Manichean work, not because it shows the relation of Nature to Spirit as one of conflict and hostility, which in fallen man it is, but because it puts the blame for this upon Nature and makes the Spirit innocent." The abstractions that have plagued Auden through some of his later poetry are around, but make out better.

In a book so titled, there is less Shakespearean criticism than one would have expected. Falstaff, Shylock, Iago are tossed about and viewed. Some of the views will strike fear into conservative hearts. "The essential Falstaff is the Falstaff of *The Merry Wives* and Verdi's opera...." On the acting of Iago: "With others, he must display every virtuoso trick of dramatic acting.... When he is alone, on the other hand, the actor must display every technical fault for which bad actors are criticized.... He must deliver the lines of his soliloquies in such a way that he makes nonsense of them." It may be a considerable time before this theatrical ideal is realized. Auden is playful. One of his plays here is the well-known essay on detective stories ("The Guilty Vicarage"). About D. H. Lawrence, Byron's Don Juan, and, less predictably, Ibsen, he is very serious. He moves easily back and forth across the Atlantic. Marianne Moore, with her animals, is paired with Lawrence, with his, in what I would agree is his most satisfying book of poems (*Birds, Beasts and Flowers*). One of Auden's rare jabs is delightful: he quotes Yeats's anthology-piece "The Scholars" and calls it "rather silly."

But much of all this is familiar to some readers in this country already. New to most of us must be his inaugural lecture at Oxford in 1956. Of many passages deserving citation, I take this:

> Speaking for myself, the questions which interest me most when reading a poem are two. The first is technical: "Here is a verbal contraption. How does it work?" The second is, in the broadest sense, moral: "What kind of a guy inhabits this poem? What is his notion of the good life or the good place? His notion of the Evil One? What does he conceal from the reader? What does he conceal even from himself?"

The modesty, the casualness, the fake-American, the Henry James, the theology, the depth-psychology, are all charmingly characteristic. Also it puts swiftly, with involuntary authority, to a good teacher, the way he has been working; or to a good reader.

PR

by Irving Howe

Little magazines are born quickly and die easily, two respects in which they differ from most human beings. For a literary journal like *Partisan Review* to have survived a quarter of a century is equivalent to a man passing the age of a hundred: he looms as a triumph of the life principle, no matter how wrinkled or bent he may now be.

Anyone who has ever undertaken the travail of editing a little magazine, struggling to cope with skeptical printers, truculent writers, and putative angels, doing by oneself at odd hours the chores that in commercial or subsidized magazines keep a paid staff busy full-time, watching with annoyance how a contributor one has nursed to modest prominence is lured away by the slicks and with rage how ideas one has fought for bitterly are in time sponged up and watered down by mass-circulation parasites who condescend to assure you that you're nice too—anyone who has gone through all this knows that William Phillips and Philip Rahv have set a record for endurance and achievement. Criticize them endlessly; but have the grace to remember that in the era of the slippery dollar they have kept alive, at some personal expense, one of the few serious literary magazines in America. A good many people who have recently made a point of sneering at *PR* would not even have been heard of if the magazine hadn't first been there to print them.

Among American literary magazines of the twentieth

century, only *The Dial* in the Twenties and *Kenyon Review* in
the Forties were so important, *The Dial* in helping to interna-
tionalize our culture by printing the major European mod-
erns, and *Kenyon* in fostering the New Criticism and its allied
poets. But *PR* not only helped establish a new school in American literature—the writers of urban, "alienated," and (in not
merely the literal sense) Jewish fiction—and a distinctive ten-
dency in American literary criticism—what might be called
the New York social critics. During its early phase the magazine also served as a center for independent radicalism among
American intellectuals; it influenced the way people thought
and felt; it kept vibrant the idea of a far-reaching, restless criticism as a style of perception, even a style of life.

In the years between 1936 and 1942 *PR* brought together
two kinds of radical sensibility, one in literature and the other
in politics. The literary avant-garde began to form in America
about the time of the First World War, as a response to the
profound cultural revolution signified by such names as Joyce,
Picasso, Schoenberg. To counter the hostility which the works
of such artists evoked in official spokesmen of culture, to find
ways of extending their innovations into American literature,
art, and music, and to insist upon the continuity between their
work and the accepted, because dead, artists of the past—this
became the task of the avant-garde. Later a section of it became politically conscious, for the aroused sensibilities that
had responded to the innovations of the modern masters now
responded to the crisis of modern society. Meanwhile, in the
middle Thirties, there was forming an unstable "independent
left," composed of intellectuals who had escaped or never en-
tered the prison-house of Stalinism, found unsatisfactory their
brief relation with the Trotskyists, but wanted to maintain, as a
value if not an ideology, the perspective of socialist renovation.

The literary avant-garde and the independent left were
not necessarily linked, and the passage of time would reveal

many points of tension between them; but for the moment there was an uneasy but fruitful union in the pages of *PR*, which led people to hope that in their own lives they also could bring together critical consciousness and political conscience.

That union has since been dissolved, and there is no likelihood it will soon be reestablished. American radicalism exists today only as an idea; the literary avant-garde is rapidly disintegrating, without clear function or assertive spirit. And the uncertainty that has followed is a major reason for the sense of drift which *PR* readers have for some years felt in its pages.

Going through the massive anthology that has recently been compiled by Phillips and Rahv from twenty-five years of the magazine, one could hardly find a clear sense of its origins or early vitality. The book is admirable; the selections, though cautious, are impressive; the distinguished names one associates with *PR* are all here: Meyer Schapiro, William Troy, Sidney Hook, Lionel Trilling, Mary McCarthy, Delmore Schwartz, Harold Rosenberg, Hannah Arendt. But alas, the anthology is a monument, not a living recreation. The rough edges, the polemical bite, the topical excitement of the early *PR* come through only occasionally in this book. What seems to be missing is the intellectual context in which the articles, reviews, and even stories were written. The tumult of the years when *PR* was fully engaged, fighting Stalinism before that became fashionable and attacking the gentility and conservatism of both the academy and certain New Critics—this barely appears in the anthology, perhaps because it no longer figures so vividly in the minds of the editors, perhaps because no mere collection can bring to life the tensions of intellectual controversy as they were once experienced.

PR quickly established its distinctive style, a mixture of polemical combativeness and intellectual rapidity, which made it influential even among those who detested its views or attacked it as "snobbish," "highbrow," and "New York provincial" (at times a euphemism for something not at all attractive). The magazine printed criticism defending modernist literature, criticism that tried to combine social range with literary faithfulness. It developed a style of reviewing quite its own: brief, ironic, fierce, sometimes rude. It cultivated the art of polemic: to fight for one's ideas meant to be alive, to care, to take risks. And it printed fiction that was sharply drawn, problematic in tone, self-consciously brilliant in style, dealing with the predicaments of urban men. The best fiction writers who first appeared in its pages—Bellow, Schwartz, Rosenfeld— transformed the local happenings of American Jewish life into a matter of "universal" bearing.

Conservative professors declared *PR* "unsound," by which they meant sometimes that its critics took extreme positions, sometimes merely that they took positions. Others charged *PR* was narrow in its interest—a charge partly irrelevant, since the magazine had as much right to confine itself to modern literature as *The Philological Quarterly* to concentrate on eighteenth-century literature, but also a charge partly valid, since *PR* had a way of getting stuck in its novelties. Still others denounced the magazine for cliquishness—a charge somewhat true but not fatal, since every editor knows that his survival depends on gathering together a group of steady contributors.

With the general postwar drift of American intellectuals toward moderation, and in response to the worldwide crisis in socialist thought, the early radicalism of *PR* began to weaken. It now seemed less irreverent, deficient in zest. It continued to publish many good things, but it could not find a sustaining idea such as had inspired its opening years. Some of the radicals who had enlivened its pages were now ex-radicals, and at times *PR* took on that peculiar sourness characterizing the disenchanted of the left, that dispirited virtuosity with which they tried to replace intellectual assurance. And in regard to strictly literary matters, the magazine was also somewhat adrift. Its earlier task of defending and analyzing the modern writers was fulfilled: Eliot, Joyce, Kafka were now absorbed, almost too well, into our cultural and academic life.

For these difficulties the editors were not entirely to blame, since they, like many others, were caught up in the intellectual crises of the time. Where *PR* did fail significantly was in responding to the rise of McCarthyism during the early Fifties. The magazine was of course opposed to McCarthy's hooliganism, but it failed to take the lead on the issue of freedom which could then once more have imbued the intellectuals with some fighting spirit. *PR*, unlike some of its New York contemporaries, did print occasional sharp attacks on the conservative drift; it did not try to minimize the badness of the situation in the name of opposing communism. But the magazine failed to speak out with enough force and persistence, or to break past the conservative hedgings of those intellectuals who led the American Committee for Cultural Freedom. The voice of the editors was barely heard in the land.

In recent years there have been signs of both trouble and renewal. *PR* remains one of our best literary magazines, even though the editors must now cope with the problem of competing with the slicks which, for reasons of their own, pay serious writers considerable sums for certain kinds of work. But *PR* suffers from a dilemma testifying to the strength of its influence upon American intellectual life. It has trained older readers to expect more than a good story here, a brilliant essay there. Its whole tradition leads them to look for intellectual guidance, for a kind of coherence no one would expect from the usual literary magazine. And but rarely do they find it.

Tenacity

by Gore Vidal

John Hersey has brought together a number of his journalistic pieces in a volume called *Here to Stay* and a baffling collection it is. To give Mr. Hersey his due—and who is so hard as not to give it him—he is good-hearted, right-minded, and, as they used to say of newspaper reporters, "tireless." He is also, as Mr. Orville Prescott would say, "dull, dull, dull." Mr. Hersey's dullness is not easily accounted for. His pieces deal with interesting subjects: Connecticut floods, concentration camp survivors, returning veterans, battle fatigue cases, and his famous *Hiroshima* study. He is fascinated by death, holocaust, and man's monotonous inhumanity to man. He can describe a disaster chastely and attentively. He has an eye for minutiae (here begins his failure for he has not much gift for selection). He is willing to take on great themes (Hiroshima), but despite his efforts, something always goes wrong. Why?

Mr. Hersey declares in his preface the hope "that this volume will give its readers a draught of adrenalin, that bitter elixer, sufficient sips of which may help put us on our guard against blunderers, tyrants, madmen and ourselves.... Drink deeply, therefore, dear reader, of the adrenal wine." Aside from the fact that adrenalin is a stimulant, not a "bitter elixir," taken by injection, not by cup, Mr. Hersey does not really invite us to do more than watch passively his newsreels of horror. He certainly does not stimulate us to right action, and there I suggest is the flaw in his method.

The Hersey technique is now a famous one. The journalist collects an immense amount of data, and then uses most of it. In one ten-line paragraph, we learn that the town of Winsted has 11,000 people, that the Mad River, swollen by water from Highland Lake, has several times washed out bridges and houses, that in '36 and '38 Main Street was flooded, and that after a flash flood on New Year's Eve ('47–'48), P. Francis Hicks, the mayor, got the Army to dredge the river at the cost of $250,000. That's a lot of fact; some is relevant, some not; none of interest in itself. Then we are told what happened at 6:10 and 7:48—Mr. Hersey has a passion for the right time and in almost every piece the time of day is given at least once… often oftener. Again why? To what end does Mr. Hersey in his level, fact-choked style insist that we attend these various disasters human and natural? So deliberately is he a camera that it is often hard to determine what he means us to feel by what is shown. The simple declarative sentences are excellent at conveying action; they are less good at suggesting atmosphere; they are hopeless at expressing a moral point of view, even by indirection.

Mr. Hersey in his prefatory note tries to provide a certain moral basis for his journalism (*e.g.*, "love can be a mortal enemy of death, especially of living death"…But is this true? Maybe. Does he prove it? In context, no.). The result is usually sententious. Yet once in a while the simple—even simple-minded— style pays off. Referring to certain Hungarian youths at the time of the uprising: "A political system is nothing more, in the end, than a system of human relationships, and what these boys understood of politics was simply that they—and all the Hungarians they knew—were being treated badly as individuals by other individuals who had taken charge of things, and they had come to believe that freedom is the sense of being treated well and that life without that sense is not worth living." Good stuff, suitable for any high-school book on "civics."

It is in Mr. Hersey's celebrated *Hiroshima* that all his virtues and faults are most revealed. He employs a familiar device of popular fiction: a number of characters are carefully described just before, during, and after a disaster, in this case the atomic bomb we dropped on a Japanese city. The material is certainly interesting, but it should be fascinating. The simple clear descriptive sentence march and march, taking the myriad facts along the way like an obstacle course. Just as one is close to pity and awe, there is a sudden injection of details: .... and *ten* nurses came in from the city of Yamaguchi with extra bandages and antiseptic, and the *third* day though another physician and a *dozen* more nurses arrived from Matuseyet, there were still only *eight* doctors for *ten thousand* patients. In the afternoon of the *third* day..." At crucial moments this numbers game is infuriating.

Of course Mr. Hersey is to be praised for avoiding emotional journalism and overt editorializing (though a week of reading Emile Zola might do him good); yet despite his properly nervous preface, he does not seem to realize that the only point to writing serious journalism is to awaken in the reader not only the sense of *how* something was, but the apprehension of *why* it was, and to what moral end the recorder is leading us, protesting or not. Mr. Hersey is content to give us mere facts. A good man, he finds war hell and human suffering terrible, but that is nowhere near enough. At no point in the deadpan monotonous chronicle of Hiroshima is there any sense of what the Bomb meant and means. He does not even touch on the public debate as to whether or not there was any need to use such a weapon when Japan was already making overtures of surrender. To Mr. Hersey it just fell, that's all, and it was terrible, and he would like to tell us about it. If he has any attitude about the moral position of the United States before and after this extraordinary human happening, he keeps it safely hidden beneath the little sentences and the small facts.

To use Mr. Hersey's own unhappy image, in reading him one does not drink the bitter elixir of adrenalin, one merely sips a familiar cup of something anodyne, something not stimulant but barbiturate, and the moral sense sleeps on.

Russian Sketches

by Alfred Kazin

This is a delicate, charming, unique record of a visit to Russia by the granddaughter of Leonid Andreyev. Mrs. Carlisle was born in Paris, and grew up in a literary atmosphere among Russian émigrés; when she saw Russia for the first time in 1960, she brought to her meetings with Soviet writers and intellectuals an intimacy with Russian culture and a particular sympathy with Russian writers as a type and as a force. Nevertheless, all this ready sympathy could not close the gap between her more traditional and idealistic Russian upbringing and the realities of Soviet life. And it is just this "literary" consciousness of old Russia in confrontation with Russia today that makes her book so vivid and sensitive as a personal record. There are odd touches of homesickness, of the kind that the children of Russian intellectuals so devoutly grow up with in exile, and notations of honest bewilderment and pain. There is a real struggle described in this book, for Mrs. Carlisle always tries to be sympathetic and fair to Russian writers (like Ehrenburg) who have had more severe trials than people in the West can appreciate. And it is the authenticity of struggle communicated in the book that makes it valuable. Many Russians of the old school go through a conflict that they cannot express.

Mrs. Carlisle, though young, is in spirit a part of "old" Russia. No doubt it is her keen "literary" consciousness of old Russia that got so many of the older Russian writers, even so brash and professionally hard a type as Mikhail Sholokhov, to talk to her so easily and richly about their work and about Soviet literature generally. She is particularly vivid on Pasternak, of course, who was himself the very embodiment of "old" intellectual Russia; but she appreciates the younger poets and painters with the same quick and informed sympathy. She has a painter's feeling for the Russian landscape and for the odd, drab, suddenly colorful life of a great anachronism like Leningrad, the beautiful city on the Neva that was the site of the Russian Revolution, but which seems to many Russians to belong to the past. There are fine touches throughout the book that bring home the amazing survival of timbered houses in the center of Moscow, the people carrying sprigs of mimosa on Sundays in winter, the hulking tyranny of the buildings of Moscow University, as overbearing as Egyptian temples. The students in the Hermitage, looking at the great paintings, walk through the rooms hand in hand, and in the long winter night Leningrad emerges as thousands of yellow lamps.

Yet the most interesting side of the book lies in the muted but expressive record of what "old" Russia can involuntarily feel in Russia today. Russia, simply as a human scene, can be difficult and oppressive enough to the complete outsider who finds himself caught up in a society where the tensions are evident, though he can never locate or understand them. But to someone like Olga Carlisle, growing up in the outside world with so many literary, highbrow, sensitive, and tender feelings about Russia, there must have been a particular shock in the recognition of how much even she, another "Russian soul," could not fully get hold of, understand, assimilate, and express. Russia has often been too much for the Russians themselves—there has been just too much space, too much winter, too much suffering, too much bureaucracy, meanness, aspiration. It can certainly be too much for a visitor, no matter how sympathetic. And not always by design, Mrs. Carlisle communicates this. She visited an émigré family that had gone back to Russia in 1947 and been promptly arrested.

The intimate familiar atmosphere made the S's tales all the more horrible. They suggested boundless injustice, immense misery, cruel endless Siberian winters, hundreds, thousands, millions of exiles.

I said good-bye to my hosts trying not to show them how upset I was. The S's live on the top floor of a dilapidated apartment house…and the staircase was barely lit, untidy. Stepping onto the snowy sidewalk I burst into sobs. The street was fortunately deserted. I walked back to the hotel, following the narrow side streets with their small log houses buried deep in snow. On the way I saw only ghostly figures of women sweeping the snow off the pavement.

Ring

by Elizabeth Hardwick

When Ring Lardner died in 1933, Scott Fitzgerald wrote an interesting and somewhat despairing tribute to him. "The point of these paragraphs is that, whatever Ring's achievement was, it fell short of the achievement he was capable of, and this because of a cynical attitude toward his work." Fitzgerald thought Lardner had developed the habit of silence about important things and that he fell back in his writing on the formulas he always had ready at hand. It is easy to imagine how this might have appeared true thirty years ago when the memory of the great short story writer working away at his daily comic strip text was still painfully near to those who cared about him. Lardner was a perplexing man, often careless about his own talents. How to account for the element of self-destroying indifference in the joshing preface to *How to Write Short Stories*, a volume that contained "My Roomy," "Champion," "Some Like Them Cold," and "The Golden Honeymoon." Edmund Wilson's review of this volume in *The Dial* spoke warmly about the stories and mentioned the disturbing unsuitability of the preface, which he found so far below Lardner's usual level that "one suspects him of a guilty conscience at attempting to disguise his talent for social observation and satire." If Lardner knew of this criticism, he was unmoved by it and introduced *The Love Nest* in a similar manner. (That volume contained, among others, "Haircut" and "Zone of Quiet.") The palpable incongruity of the jocular prefaces as an introduction to the superlatively bitter stories serves as a mirror to the strangeness of Lardner's personality and work.

Reading Lardner again now is almost a new experience. Somewhat unexpectedly one finds that he has a dismal cogency to a booming America: his subjects are dishonesty, social climbing, boastfulness, and waste. For that reason, Maxwell Geismar's new collection is valuable as a way of bringing Lardner once more to public notice. This new volume, because of larger print, is easier to read than the Viking *Portable Ring Lardner*, but it is not otherwise an improvement. Indeed the Viking *Portable* has the advantage of the complete text of "You Know Me, Al" and "The Big Town." Geismar's preface does not supply more than the usual demand; nevertheless his selection will not fail anyone who wants the unsettling experience of discovering Ring Lardner or of rediscovering him.

Out of a daily struggle to make a living by literary work of various kinds, Lardner produced many short stories and some longer works of great originality. These stories were also immensely popular and nothing touches us more than this rare happening. In a country like ours where there will necessarily be so much journalism, so much support of the popular, the successful, we are naturally unusually grateful when we find the genuine among the acceptable. And with Lardner there is something more: he made literature out of baseball, the bridge game, and the wisecrack. Of course he was terribly funny, but even in his funniest stories there is a special desolation, a sense of national emptiness filled by stupidity and vanity.

Now, in the 1960s, the distance from the 1920s reduces some of the journalistic aspects of Lardner's writing. We are struck most of all by his difference from popular writing today. His is a miserable world made tolerable only by a ma-

niacal flow of wisecracks. "That's Marie Antoinette's bed,"
the four-flusher says as he shows a couple around his River-
side Drive apartment. The wisecracker asks, "What time does
she usually get in it?" When the wife says, "Guess who called
me today?" the husband answers, "Josephus Daniels or Henry
Ford. Or maybe it was the guy with the scar on his lip that you
thought was smiling at you the other day." Out of the plain,
unabashed gag, and the cruel dialogue of domestic life, Lardner created his odd stories, with their curious speed, rush of
situation, explosion of insult and embarrassment.

Lardner's characters have every mean fault, but they lack
the patience to do much with their meanness. The busher is
boastful and stingy, and yet utterly unable, for all his surface
shrewdness, to discover his real place in the scheme of things.
He is always being dropped by the women he had boasted
about and all his stinginess cannot help to manage his affairs.
Lardner's stories are filled with greedy, grasping people who
nevertheless go bankrupt. You cannot say they are cheated,
since they are themselves such awful cheats. The Gullibles
have the fantastic idea of going to Palm Beach to get into
"society." Mrs. Gullible does at last meet Mrs. Potter Palmer
in the corridor of the hotel and Mrs. Palmer asks her to put
more towels in her suite. The squandering of an inheritance
by the characters in "The Big Town" shows a complete lack
of elementary common sense. The husbands usually have
some idea of the cost of things and of the absurdity of their
wives' ambitions. But they cannot act upon their knowledge.
It comes out only in the constant static of their wisecracks.
Wildly joking, they go along with their wives into debt
and humiliation. It is hard to feel much sympathy and yet
occasionally one does so: the sympathy comes, when it does,
from the fact that the jokes played upon these dreadful
people are after all thoroughly real and mean. Even the language they speak with such immense, dismaying humor is a

kind of joke on real language, funnier and more cutting than we can bear.

Vanity, greed, and cruel humor are the themes of Lardner's stories. The lack of self-knowledge is made up for by a dizzy readiness with cheap alibis. No group or class seems better than another; there is a democracy of cheapness and shallowness. Lies are at the core of nearly every character he produces for us. The only fear is being caught out, exposed to the truth. Love cannot exist because the moment it runs into trouble the people lie about their former feelings. Because of the habit of lying, it is a world without common sense. The tortured characters are not always victims. They may be ruined and made fun of, but they have the last word. They bite the leg that kicks them.

"Haircut" is one of the cruelest pieces of American fiction. Even Lardner seems to have felt some need for relief from the relentless evil of the small-town joker and so he has him killed in the end. This cruel story is just about the only one that has the contrast of decent people preyed upon by a maniac. "Champion" is brutal and "The Golden Honeymoon" is a masterpiece of grim realism. Alfred Kazin speaks of the "harsh, glazed coldness" of Lardner's work. He wrapped his dreadful events in comic language, as you would put an insecticide in a bright can.

Lardner's personality is very difficult to take hold of. In spite of poor health that came, so far as I can discover, from his devastating drinking, he had the continuing productivity of the professional journalist. He went to work every morning. Why he drank, why his views were so bitter are a mystery. He came from a charming, talented family and married a woman he loved. He was kind, reserved, hard-working; his fictional world is loud, cruel, filled with desperate marriages, hideous old age, suburban wretchedness, fraud, drunkenness. Even the sports world is degraded and athletes are likely to be sadists, crooks, or dumbbells. The vision is thoroughly desperate. All the literature of the 1930s and 1940s does not contain such pure subversion, snatched on the run from the common man and his old jokes.

New Editions

by William Styron

I can recall with clarity from childhood my North Carolina grandmother's reminiscences of her slaves. To be sure, she was an old lady well into her eighties at the time, and had been a young girl growing up during the Civil War when she owned human property. Nonetheless, that past is linked to our present by a space of time which is startlingly brief. The violent happenings that occur in Oxford, Mississippi, do not take place in a vacuum of the moment but are attached historically to slavery itself. That in the Commonwealth of Virginia there is a county today in which no Negro child has been allowed to attend school for over four years has far less relevance to Senator Byrd than to the antebellum Black Laws of Virginia, which even now read like the code of regulations from an inconceivably vast and much longer enduring Nazi concentration camp.

As Professor Stanley Elkins has pointed out, the scholarly debate over slavery has for nearly a century seesawed with a kind of topheavy, contentious, persistent rhythm, the rhythm of "right" and "wrong." These points of view, shifting between the Georgia-born historian Ulrich Phillips's vision of the plantation slave as an essentially cheerful, childlike, submissive creature who was also in general well-treated (a viewpoint which, incidentally, dominated historical scholarship for the decades between the two World Wars) and Kenneth Stampp's more recent interpretation of American slavery (*The Peculiar*

Institution) as a harsh and brutal system, practically devoid of any charity at all, have each been so marred by a kind of moral aggression and self-righteousness as to resemble, in the end, a debate between William Lloyd Garrison and John C. Calhoun—and we have had enough of such debates. Granted that it seems inescapable that the plantation slave, at least, often displayed a cheerful, childlike, and submissive countenance, and that plantation life had its sunny aspects; granted, too, that the system was at heart incredibly brutal and inhumane, the question remains: Why? Why was American slavery the unique institution that it was? What was the tragic essence of this system which still casts its shadow not only over our daily life, but over our national destiny as well? Professor Frank Tannenbaum's brief work, *Slave and Citizen: The Negro in the Americas*, first published by Knopf in 1948 and reprinted this month under the Vintage imprint, is a modest but important attempt to answer these questions.

Tannenbaum's technique is that of comparison—the comparison of slavery in the United States with that of coexisting slave systems in Latin America. Slavery was introduced by the Spanish and Portuguese into South America at the identical moment that it was brought to North America and the West Indies by the British, and its duration in time as an institution on both continents was roughly the same. But it is a striking fact that today there is no real racial "problem" in Brazil; a long history of miscegenation has blurred the color line, legal sanctions because of race do not exist, and any impediments toward social advancement for the Negro are insignificant. That this is true is due to an attitude toward slavery which had become crystallized in the Portuguese and Spanish ethic even before slaves were brought to the shores of the New World. For slavery (including the slavery of white people), as Tannenbaum points out, had existed on the Iberian peninsula throughout the fourteenth and fifteenth centuries.

Oppressive an institution as it may have been, it contained large elements of humanity, even of equality, which had been the legacy of the Justinian Code. Thus Seneca: "A slave can be just, brave, magnanimous." *Las Sieste Partidas*, the body of law which evolved to govern all aspects of slavery, not only partook of the humanitarian traditions of the Justinian Code, but was framed within that aspect of Christian doctrine which regarded the slave as the spiritual equal of his master, and perhaps his better. The law was protective of the slaves, and in conjunction with the Church provided many incentives for freedom; and this attitude persisted when Negro slavery was established in South America. Despite its frequent brutality, the institution of slavery in Brazil, with its recognition of the slave as a moral human being, and its bias in favor of manumission, had become in effect, as Tannenbaum says, "a contractual arrangement between the master and his bondsman and in such a relatively agreeable atmosphere it is not unnatural that full liberty was attained through a slow and genial mingling of the races, and by gradual change rather than through such a cataclysm as Civil War."

We are only beginning to realize the extent to which American slavery worked its psychic and moral devastation upon an entire race. Unlike the Spanish and the Portuguese, the British and their descendants who became American slaveowners had no historical experience of slavery; and neither the Protestant church nor Anglo-American law was equipped to cope with the staggering problem of the status of the Negro: forced to choose between regarding him as a moral human being and as property, they chose the definition of property. The result was the utter degradation of a people. Manumission was totally discouraged. A slave became only a negotiable article of goods, without rights to property, to the products of his own work, to marriage, without rights even to the offspring of his own despairing, unsanctioned unions—

all of these were violations of the spirit so shattering as to beg the question whether the white South was populated either by tolerant, amiable Marse Bobs or by sadistic Simon Legrees. Even the accounts of brutality (and it is difficult even now, when witnessing the moral squabble between those historians who are apologists and those who are neo-abolitionists, to tell whether brutality was insignificant or rampant) fade into inconsequence against a backdrop in which the total dehumanization of a race took place, and a systematic attempt, largely successful, was made to reduce an entire people to the status of children. It was an oppression unparalleled in human history. In the end only a Civil War could try to rectify this outrage, and the war came too late.

> In Latin America the Negro achieved complete legal equality slowly, through manumission, over centuries, and after he had acquired a moral personality. In the United States he was given his freedom suddenly, and before the white community credited him with moral status.

That is the problem we are faced with today: too many white Americans still deny the Negro his position as a moral human being.

Unfortunately, history does not give answers to the problems it leaves us. Professor Tannenbaum concludes his excellent study with the reasonable implication that the attainment by the Negro of a moral status may still take a very long time. It seems apparent that a very long time might be too long for our salvation.

New Editions

by Jason Epstein

The Heritage Press has reissued in three volumes its indispensable edition of Gibbon's *Decline and Fall of the Roman Empire*, with an introduction by the late Professor Bury and with his version of the text. This edition had long been out of print, available only sporadically on the secondhand market at about fifty dollars. The Heritage Press edition is to be commended for its handsome and clear typography and design in which Gibbon's notes appear, as they should, in the margins of each page adjacent to the textual passages which they are meant to amplify.

It is unfortunate, on the other hand, that the publishers chose to illustrate their edition with engravings by Piranesi who, though he was Gibbon's contemporary, approaches Roman antiquity in a somewhat more valetudinarian spirit than Gibbon would have liked. Furthermore, Piranesi's engravings, which show the antiquities as they appeared in the eighteenth century, half-buried and often in ruins, surrounded by contemporary buildings and out of scale, are, for all their brilliance, hardly as illuminating as reconstructions of the original states of these monuments would have been and still less illuminating than reproductions of the coins, medals, and trophies to which Gibbon continually refers and on which his argument so greatly depends. Finally, the publishers have chosen to print the engravings in a brown tone rather than in Piranesi's own black, with the result that the reproductions are not at all representative of the originals.

It is also to be regretted that the publishers did not take this opportunity to replace Philip Guedalla's introduction, which was no good to begin with and is now hopelessly out of date, with something more apposite and scholarly. This new printing might also have been the occasion to give Professor Bury's admirable text, which is now many years old, to a modern scholar for further emendation.

Nevertheless, the new edition, whatever its faults—and these include the binding, which is too flimsy for volumes this large—is the best we have and perhaps the best we shall have for some time to come. It is to be hoped, however, that in future printings the publishers will replace the present endpaper maps, which are very sparse, with maps that are more informative.

Robert Frost: 1874-1963

by Robert Lowell

After Frost's wife died in the Thirties, he stepped up the pace of his public readings. He must have gotten consolation from being Robert Frost, from being the image of himself that he had perfected with such genius. I have heard him say mockingly that hell was a half-filled auditorium. This was a hell he never had to suffer. Year after year after year, he was as great a drawing-card as Dylan Thomas was in his brief prime. Yet there was a strain; never in his life was he able to eat before a reading. A mutual friend of ours once said with pity, "It's sad to see Frost storming about the country when he might have been an honest schoolteacher."

Frost had an insatiable yearning for crowds, circles of listeners, single listeners—and even for solitude. Can we believe him when he says he "took the road less travelled by"? He ran, I think, in no tracks except the ones he made for himself. The thinker and poet that most influenced him was Emerson. Both had something of the same highly urbane yet homemade finish and something of the same knack for verbal discovery. Both went about talking. Both leaned on and defied the colleges. A few of their poems are almost interchangeable. "In May when sea winds pierced our solitudes—I found the fresh Rhodora in the woods." Part of Frost was wary of Emerson. "Great is the art / Great shall be the manners of the bard." He knew better than anyone that his neighbors would find this manner boring and insufferable. He tried to make himself a man of many

ruses, subtle surprises, and weathered agility. He was almost a
farmer. Yet under the camouflage there was always the
Brahma crouching, a Whitman, a great-mannered bard. If God
had stood in his sunlight, he would have elbowed God away
with a thrust or a joke.

He wasn't quite a farmer even in his early, isolated years.
He didn't quite make a living; he got up at noon. He said the
cows got used to his hours more easily than his neighbors.
There was nothing very heroic or out of the ordinary here, yet
these fifteen years or so of farming were as valuable to him as
Melville's whaling or Faulkner's Mississippi. Without exactly
knowing it, and probably not intending it, Frost found he was
different from other men of letters. He used to tell a story
about a Florida train trip he took with Wallace Stevens. The
two poets were nervous with each other. Stevens however was
more in the vacationer's mood. He made witty remarks, and
finally said, "The trouble with your poetry, Frost, is that it has
subjects." I don't want to spoil the weird, whimsical rightness of
Stevens's taunt. Frost had an unfashionable hold on subjects.
What were they?

I suppose what I liked about Frost's poems when I read
them thirty years ago was their description of the New England
country, a world I knew mostly from summer and weekend
dips into it. It was a boy's world, fresher, grainer, tougher, and
freer than the city where I had to live. "Back out of all this now
too much for us," "Over back there where they speak of life as
staying," "the dory filled to the gunnels with flowers," "the tar-
banded ancient cherry trees," one man saying, "Weren't you re-
lived to find he wasn't dead?" and the other answering, "No!
and yet I don't know—it's hard to say / I went about to kill him
fair enough." I used to wonder if I knew anything about the
country that wasn't in Frost. I always had the pleasure of either
having my own knowledge confirmed or learning something
new that completed it. I hardly cared which.

The arts do not progress but move along by surges and sags. Frost, born in 1874, was our last poet who could honestly ignore the new techniques that were to shatter the crust. He understood the use of tools, often wonderful tools, that five or ten years later would be forever obsolete. He was a continuer and completer and not a copyist. When he began to write the American cultural scene was unimaginably different from anything we now know. There were no celebrated masters to meet, no one to imitate. Poetry was the great English Romantics and Victorians and their famous, official American offshoots. Through their practice, criticism, and translations, the known past had been reborn in their image.

Frost had a hundred years' tradition he could accept without question, yet he had to teach himself everything. Excellence had left the old poetry. Like the New England countryside, it had run through its soil and had been dead a long time. Frost rebuilt both the soil and the poetry: by edging deeper and deeper into the country and its people, he found he was possessed by the old style. He became the best strictly metered poet in our history, and our best local observer, at least in meter. The high wind of inspiration blew through his long, packed, isolated rustication. By the time he was forty and had finished his second book, *North of Boston*, he had arrived. Step by step, he had tested his observation of places and people until his best poems had the human and seen richness of great novels. No one had helped him to learn, and now no one could because no one wrote better.

Randall Jarrell has a fine phrase about Frost's "matter-of-fact magnificence." He writes that the poems' subjects are isolation, extinction, and the learning of human limitation. These three themes combine, I think, in a single main theme, that of a man moving through the formless, the lawless and the free, of moving into snow, air, ocean, waste, despair, death, and madness. When the limits are reached, and sometimes almost passed, the man returns.

This is what I remember about Frost. There was music in his voice, in the way he made his quotations ring, in the spin on his language, in the strange, intuitive waywardness of his toleration. He was less of the specialized literary man than other poets and more curious personally.

Last November I walked by his house on Brewster Street in Cambridge. Its narrow gray wood was a town cousin of the farmhouses he wrote about, and stood on some middle ground between luxury and poverty. It was a traveler from the last century that had inconspicuously drifted over the customs border of time. Here one night he was talking about the suicide of a young friend, and said that sometimes when he was excited and full of himself, he came back by thinking how little good his health could do those who were close to him.

The lights were out that night; they are out for good now, but I can easily imagine the barish rooms, the miscellaneous gold-lettered old classics, the Georgian poets, the Catullus by his bedside, the iron stove where he sometimes did his cooking, and the stool drawn up to his visitor's chair so that he could ramble and listen.

FMF

by Allen Tate

From 1927 to the year before his death in 1939 I knew Ford very well, as well as a man so much younger could have known him. I knew him first in New York, where he had for a few months rooms in a brownstone house in Perry Street in which I had a free apartment in exchange for being the janitor. In the winter of 1929, while he was in the United States again, he lent us his flat in Paris at 32 rue de Vaugirard. In the Thirties he visited me several times in Tennessee, first at Memphis, and then at my farm near Clarksville where in the summer of 1937 he wrote much of *The March of Literature*. In that summer he brought with him his wife Janice Biala, the painter, and her sister-in-law, Mrs. Jack Tworkov, his secretary; Robert Lowell lived in a tent on the lawn, where he intoned the Miltonic blank verse that he wrote every morning. My wife Caroline Gordon, with one idiotic servant, ran the precariously balanced *ménage*. Ford could eat French food only, but Ida, with the occasional assistance of her mother Electra, the washerwoman, could not even cook Tennessee, much less French. Ford was unhappy in the 95°F. but every morning he paced the columned gallery—which had nothing but the earth to support it—and dictated to Mrs. Tworkov several pages of *The March of Literature*. There was a persistent tide that seldom ebbed, of visitors from Nashville, from Louisville, from New York, from Europe. It was a situation perversely planned by fate to expose human weakness. There were no scenes. Were

we not, like the Ashburnhams and the Dowells, "quite good
people"? Yet much became known to us about one another
that we could have written, as "trapped spectators," of what
might have happened but didn't.

After Ford's death I began to feel that I had perhaps written a novel that I had put away and all but forgotten: had written it as the trapped spectator John Dowell in *The Good
Soldier*, who "knew Edward very well" but then at last knew
nothing at all about him. To this day I know nothing of Ford,
except his great kindness to me as a young man. Ford's biographers at their peril will set up as omniscient narrators: they
will have to assume the role of Dowell, the hesitant prober of
motive with the intimate but obfuscated view, and through
progressions d'effet come out in the end with the image but
not the essence of the man. For he was a character in one of
his own later novels. Will not his "method" be the best one
possible for his biographers? His conversation either illus-
trated or was the source of his theory of fictional dialogue. Dialogue must never convey information; it may be about
nothing at all so long as it is in character. ("Just might do it,"
says Ashburnham on a polo field. "Shuttlecocks!" says Nancy
Rufford repeatedly.) Ford's casual observations could be de-
tached from their occasions without loss of meaning, for he
always spoke in character.

I remember a fine evening in Paris in the autumn of 1928
when I was walking with him by the Petit Luxembourg, and he
suddenly spoke, as if to himself (as Ashburnham seems always
to speak): "One might be a peer of the realm or a member of
the Académie Française. There is nothing else." It had no
"context." Was it really as fatuous as it sounded? I think not.
John Dowell would have let the remark drop casually, but with
shocking force, and then through some thirty pages of "time-
shifts" show how it came out of the total "affair" which was
Ford's life. We shall never know much more *of* Ford— how-

ever much his biographers may find out *about* him—than the brief self-revelation which reveals little. Ford, like Ashburnham and Tietjens, will be made "known" to us through the Jamesian-Fordian technique of "gradual revelation" and *progression d'effet*, by which we will witness the "affair," the significant action of a given moment of history, and then the pathos which will fall just a little short of tragedy, as *The Good Soldier* falls short of tragic action. And why should this be so? It is Ford's great theme that tragic action must be incomplete in a world that does not allow the hero to take the full Oedipean responsibility for the evil that he did not intend but that he has nevertheless done.

What I am trying to say is that Ford's best biographer will understand at the outset that Ford himself must be approached as a character in a novel, and that novel a novel by Ford. The complaint, often heard today, that James, Conrad, and Ford were each in his own degree obsessed by "form" or "method" is of course nonsense; but if it were true, would it be less damaging to the vitality of the novel in our day than the obsession with the expressionistic egotism and disorder of American novelists since the War? Ford was not, in the pejorative sense, a formalist. Ford's technique is Ford, and he could have had no other. So the biographer must collect and compare the views—as Dowell collects and compares—of Jessie Conrad and Violet Hunt, and attend closely to the correction of these views by Mr. Douglas Goldring, whose two books, *South Lodge* and *Trained for Genius*, though necessarily incomplete in documentation, will have to be accepted as the Ford primers by their more scholarly successors. Mr. Goldring knew Ford "well," but being the younger man could not have been in the action of the novel which was Ford's life. He will probably remain the best contemporaneous witness.

There are now in print three large critical studies of Ford which are the ostensible subject of this article. Mr. Cassell, Mr.

Meixner, and Mr. Wiley—each has his particular insight; we shall remain permanently in their debt. I must have read *The Good Soldier* some thirty-five times; I imitated it, in the way Johnson imitated Juvenal in *London*, in a novel I wrote about twenty-five years ago. My novel might have been better had I understood the construction of *The Good Soldier* as shrewdly as Mr. Cassell does: that, I think, is Mr. Cassell's virtue—his grasp of the symmetries and correspondences of form. Mr. Meixner is, I believe, more than his rival colleagues, sensitive to the nuances of Ford's style: its great flexibility, its tightrope virtuosity which combines colloquial rhythms and idioms with high eloquence. For this reason he understands better than anybody I have read the role of Dowell in *The Good Soldier*; it is his awareness of what style does in this great novel that enables him to put Mr. Mark Schorer's Introduction to the Vintage edition out of court. Mr. Schorer suggests that the novel is a comedy of humor, the humor being phlegm, because Dowell is passive and obtuse. I am surprised that a critic of Mr. Schorer's experience could take a personal narrator at his word; I surmise that he would believe everything that the Governess says about what she thinks is happening in *The Turn of the Screw*. Through subtle shifts of tone Dowell brings to bear upon the "affair" two points of view, his own and that of Ford, who is standing over his shoulder: the tragic action is delineated by Ford (through Dowell's eyes); the irony of this action is established by Dowell's faltering perception of it; and Dowell is the world. It is as if *Oedipus Rex* were a novel told in the first person by Creon. The action would be the same, but our access to the action would be delayed by Creon's limited perception. Mr. Wiley's book is less concerned than the two others with style and form, but his book is nevertheless a valuable addition to our understanding of Ford. His object is to show Ford's development from the early novels, up to *The Good Soldier* and through *Parade's End* to the decline in a late work like *When the Wicked Man:* this development is simply an increasing sense of the "affair" most deeply significant of the shift from decadent aristocracy to middle-class liberalism, along with a sharper sense of the fictional techniques best adapted to render the affair in its complete objectivity. All three of our critics agree that *The Good Soldier* offers us the most nearly perfect fusion of subject and method.

Besides these three books, there is also the formidable bibliography of Ford's writings and of writings about Ford, by Mr. David Low Harvey. Mr. Harvey lists 1,033 titles beginning with a review of *The Brown Owl* in the London *Times* in 1891 and ending with Richard Foster's essay on *Zeppelin Nights* in *The Minnesota Review* of Summer 1962. Since the Second World War the number of articles about Ford has increased yearly at a rate that suggests geometrical progression; and it must also be said that there has been an increase not only in quantity but in the informed intelligence paid him. Recent studies and reviews of Ford, with the exception of the prefaces and articles by Graham Greene and Caroline Gordon, are by younger writers who could not have known Ford *en pantoufles* and who are not blinded by the fog or war that settled upon his reputation after the affair with Violet Hunt and the attacks upon him for his version of the collaboration with Conrad. If the essays published so far by Richard W. Lid and Richard M. Ludwig are parts of books yet to appear, as I hear they are, there will shortly be five books about Ford since 1961. There is still in manuscript a biography by Frank McShane; and another biography, which I understand will have the full support of Miss Janice Biala, who owns the letters and other private papers, will appear in the next few years from the hand of Mr. Arthur Mizener. If this book comes out, say, by 1966, and Mr. McShane's not much later than that, there will have been by 1966 seven full-length biographies and critical studies of Ford within five years. The staggering disproportion between the number of books about Ford and the number of his own books that may then be in print will be an anomaly of Anglo-American literary history. It will be easier to read about Ford than to read him.

Is it possible that all these studies will inspire publishers to lose money by getting back into print the minor works, and to sacrifice themselves in an heroic effort to hush up the scandal of this anomaly? Ford knew a great deal about scandal, but this sort never came within his purview. I think that the irony might have pleased him, but he would say, were he alive, as he often said about matters that he didn't want to discuss, "I am too old and too distinguished to think about it."

The future of his reputation is further complicated by the critical distinction of the three books so far published. This may trap us in the illusion that there is a Ford revival. There may be one soon, if Mr. Greene's plan to republish Ford, a few books a year, meets with any success at all. But for the moment only a few scholars and critics will be introduced to Ford, and his old admirers edified, by the three books here under review. It is not likely that the general reader (if he exists) will get further than hearing about them.

Guided Tour

by Alfred Chester

This is the worst confection yet devised by the masterminds behind the Grove *épater-la-post-office* Machine. So fabricated is it that, despite the adorable photograph on the rear of the dust jacket, I can hardly believe there is a real John Rechy — and if there is, he would probably be the first to agree that there isn't—for *City of Night* reads like the unTrue Confessions of a Male Whore as told to Jean Genet, Djuna Barnes, Truman Capote, Gore Vidal, Thomas Wolfe, Fanny Hurst, and Dr. Franzblau. It is pastiche from the word go. Here are three quotes that come to you through the courtesy of page 1 alone:

> Later I would think of America as one vast City of Night stretching gaudily from Times Square to Hollywood Boulevard—jukebox-winking, rock-n-roll moaning: America at night fusing its dark cities into the unmistakable shape of loneliness.
>
> One night sex and cigarette smoke and rooms squashed in by loneliness....
>
> And I would remember lives lived out darkly in that vast City of Night, from all-night movies to Beverly Hills mansions.

Actually, *City of Night* is two books of short stories, sneaking their way through each other to give the volume the appearance of a novel, partly, I would guess, because novels are more negotiable than short stories and partly, I am sure, because the amorality of the characters in what I will call Book One helps disguise the eminently respectable morality of the hero-narrator in Book Two. The episodes that comprise Book One are concerned with those lives lived out darkly in what is nowadays called The Homosexual Underground, though never before has it been so much on the surface. We are taken on a guided tour of gay bars and beaches, Turkish baths, parks, S & M scenes (sadomasochism for those of you who aren't aficionados), queer parties and movie houses, faggot social life and street life, and so on. The works. It is a blow by blow account, so to speak, of where to go for what you want (assuming of course that you want it)—a kind of "Sodom on Five Dollars a Day." Throughout most of these episodes, the nameless hero of the novel plays no part except as observer or listener; his passport into this world that never, finally, makes him is the fact that he's a hustler and lets himself be had for money. (I regret telling you that the full extent or the exact nature of his being had is something he and Rechy are quite silent about.) These stories do not bring anything new to literature, homosexual, sociological, or American. They're mostly about the same old queens doing the same old things: swishing and bitching and cruising and falling in love and leaving each other and getting desperate and growing old and worrying over it. And there's no general reason why it shouldn't be pleasant to read about them once again. But Rechy's stories are awful, and they're awful for two very specific reasons which may ultimately sound like one. The first is that disgusting rhetoric that Rechy pours all over everything like jam. The episodes are so gracelessly, clumsily written, so stickily, thickly literary; in his determination to boil every last drop of poetry out of pederasty, Rechy ends up with nothing but a pot of blackberry prose. The trouble is, he has no ear whatsoever. He is deaf to the music in language, and thus deaf to the rhythms of homosexual speech. He is not, however, deaf to the fact that other writers haven't been, and through their ears he listens to his own characters.

Here is Rechy listening though Capote listening through Djuna Barnes:

> For me something does indeed shine: the wings of the angels—briefly but clearly. Angels are all I see when I glance heavenward, and that is Enough. And? I never know how I shall meet those angels—it was not always as it is now—when Larry chooses them for me. You see, I am bedridden.... Sometimes he brings me demi-angels: they last only one interview. But sometimes there are jewels in the streets.

And here is Rechy listening through Jean Genet:

> Indeed, indeed! here comes Miss Destiny! fluttering out of the shadows into the dimlights along the ledges like a giant firefly—flirting, calling out to everyone: "Hello, darling, I love you—I love you too, dear—so very much— ummm !" Kisses flung recklessly into the wind.... "What oh what did Chuck say to you, darling?" to me, coming on breathlessly rushing. "You must understand right here and now that Chuck still loves me, like all my exhusbands (youre new in town, dear, or I would certainly have seen you before, and do you have a place to stay?—I live on Spring Street and there is a 'Welcome!' mat at the door)....

Like all false poets, Rechy listens to other poets and not to life, and like all false poets, he tries to make poetry out of mood rather than music. And he tries it with all the conventional contemporary props. He is full of "night" and "loneliness." He is full of "dark" and "fireflies" and "shadows." He is full of "wind." But he is utterly void of song. So his stories give you the feeling that you have heard them before and don't want to hear them again, and the feeling is even stronger in the episodes whose original teller you can't identify than in those whose you can.

The second, and perhaps more internal, reason for Rechy's failure in Book One is that there is absolutely no real, living response in the narrator to the things and people he talks about and witnesses. This is not merely the result of a suspension of judgment or moral attitude; it isn't this at all. It is a terrified refusal by the hero—or if I may say so, by the author—to respond honestly and immediately lest the response be construed (if only by himself) as an involvement. This is very much in keeping with the nature of the hero who wants to limit his homosexual life to where he wears his BVDs—no love an' kisses, man, cause I'm butch, man—and if his author had let him be, it might have proved interesting. But Rechy must have read a book of rules and regulations somewhere and learned that characters have got to respond in order to be lifelike. So he makes his poor frightened hustler respond, but not as a man, as a writer—and everyone on earth knows that writers don't feel, they just talk. The hustler, then, substitutes literature for emotion, as in that "Indeed, indeed" nonsense quoted above. This results in the total castration of humor and life, even that little bit of it that might have crept in if the hero never tried to respond and merely described things flatly, with his own, or his author's, inhibitions in open operation. Rechy has too little confidence, is too scared, to give himself to the public as he is, however good or bad that may be, so he coats himself with literary armor before sallying out into the world. This would be innocence if one did not feel he had begun to confuse himself with his armor—and that of course would be corruption.

Book Two of *City of Night* is a series of love stories in which the narrator is the beloved and unwilling participant.

He wants to be loved and wanted, but he doesn't want to love or want—he doesn't, in fact, want to be queer, though this is much too chic a book to admit that except backhandedly. Our hero is a very loveless boy, the kind of person we now speak of as "someone incapable of love." And, as with all these people, if you are hot for them enough, or bedeviled and tormented by them enough, and if you look and examine very hard, you will find that it is not at all true that they cannot love. They can; they do; alas, they love too much, which is the problem, for they are always loving someone else. They too are hot, bedeviled, and tormented; they too are looking and examining— even if their object is only a dead mother, a brother, a boyhood chum grown fat and foul. Rechy's hero loves his mother and hates his father or something like that and is spending his youth in a Freudian way making men pay, literally and emotionally, for his dull parental complexes. (There is also some big narcissism complex he's got which I'm too lazy to figure out.) What it all adds up to is another tale about another boy who won't surrender to his homosexuality. Instead of the usual puritan ethic, Rechy uses Freudian psychology, but it's still the same old baloney. All his abortive love affairs are written out of the traditional anguished, romantic sentimentality, and of course you wish, you just wish like mad that sodomy wasn't against the laws of heaven and earth so this sweet little whore could make it for life with some nice guy—settle down to a pretty house in the suburbs, regular job, TV, kids with corn-colored hair. But even here the lump in the throat keeps getting Reched out by the author's literary bent. Everything has to get written down. The last of these romantic episodes takes place in a bedroom in New Orleans, Mardi Gras time, of course, with raging Inferno images everywhere, of course. Our hero has been rented by a "well-built, masculine man in his early thirties, with uncannily dark eyes, light hair. He is intensely, moodily handsome.... Looking at him, I wonder why such a man

would pay another male when he could obviously make it easily and mutually in any of the bars." (The reason why is soon
made clear to the reader, but not to the narrator, and certainly
not to the author who is always so busy writing that he is the
last one to know what his characters are like. The man has to
pay because he is so boring that no one in his right mind would
spend more than five minutes talking to him gratis.) The ensu-
ing bedroom conversation, covering nearly twenty-five pages,
is surely the most lengthy and embarrassing exposition of
Franzblauthink ever to appear outside the pages of *The New
York Post*.

"You want, very much, to be loved—but you don't
want to love back, even if you have to force yourself not
to."

...I grab defensively for the streetpose that will dismiss his statement. "Oh, man, dig," I said, "I just want to
ball while I can."

"Wouldn't your masculinity be compromised much
less if you tested your being 'wanted' with women instead
of men?"

"It's easier to hustle men," I defended myself
quickly.

"I think it's something else," he went on relentlessly.
"Even a wayward revenge on your own sex—your father's sex....

"I'm sure youve thought you have a definite advantage of whatever kind over the people youve been with,
because theyve wanted *you*, because theyve paid *you*—
some sort of victory beyond the sex-experience, beyond
the money. (But don't *you* need *them* just as badly?)....
And it's not just on your side that the symbols take over
and create the elaborate guilt-ridden defenses."

This, I want you to know, is supposed to be courtship, for

Jeremy, as the man with the uncannily dark eyes is called, wants to marry the hustler in spite of her past. It is a near miss for both of them, since our hero does what he has apparently never done before to any other man: he kisses Jeremy on the lips.

> And I was thinking: Yes, maybe youre right. Maybe I could love you. But I won't.
>
> The grinding streets awaited me.

But he doesn't stay on the grinding streets very long. Mardi Gras is hardly over when he suddenly undergoes a page-and-a-half of religious conversion, telephoning churches all over town, and that symbolical sine qua non taken care of, he returns home to El Paso and Mama.

> Here, by another window, I'll look back on the world and I'll try to understand.... But, perhaps, mysteriously, it's all beyond reason. Perhaps it's as futile as trying to capture the wind.

Oooo, Mary, doesn't it make chills go up and down your spine? Especially with all those apostrophes mysteriously shoved back into their contractions!

So the hustler goes home to Texas, still pure as the driven prairies. He hasn't surrendered to the crime against nature, to the sin that has no name—just like a good American boy shouldn't. His virtue is intact because he never loved no one but Mama, and his masculinity is whole because it was never punctured except for money. How interesting that lovelessness and prostitution should, without any evidence of irony, serve Rechy's work as saviors of puritanism and middle-class moral-ity. If it weren't so deadpan, it would be a scream. But the only sense of humor in or around *City of Night* comes from the guy who wrote the jacket blurb: "This is a novel about America. It is a novel about loneliness, about love and the ceaseless, groping search for love."

Better cut out all that ceaseless groping, Jack, and get down to work!

Longfellow

by Richard Wilbur

After his second wife's horrible death by fire, in 1861, Longfellow's face was too seared to be shaven, and he grew a beard. It was this beard in which he was received by Queen Victoria, toasted by Gladstone, and seen by a vast international public as the foremost of American poets. For those of us who were taught in grade school to revere him and in college to shrug him off, the beard is an obstacle to fresh acquaintance, and Newton Arvin has wisely chosen a frontispiece in which the forty-eight-year-old man is obscured only by burnsides. What the photograph shows, immediately, is the "lit-up face and glowing warmth and courtesy" which Whitman encountered. But that we might have guessed: less expected is the general air of robust youthfulness. In the lift of the head, in the strong brows and nose, there is a look of romantic adventurousness, or perhaps, as Mr. Arvin suggests, of command. The eyes are direct, clear, and full of life, though a pronounced fold at the outer corners gives them a touch of sadness. The mouth, in contradiction to all that may seem rugged in the other feature, is generous, comfort-loving, and a bit unformed.

Like the frontispiece, Mr. Arvin's excellent account of Longfellow's life presents the man rather than the idol. This is not to say that the biographical chapters confer any illusion of intimacy with Longfellow; the proportions of the study permit very little detail, very little quotation from journal or letters; the method is neither dramatic nor atmospheric, and we do not fancy that we are "there." We do, however, gain from Mr. Arvin's spare, pointed narrative a just perspective on a unique career, and an admirably reserved interpretation of a character which was less simple than it seemed.

Few writers have been so fortunate. Longfellow suffered three painful bereavements, but the rest of his life was incessantly sweet. He was born into a cultured, comfortable family of good standing, and brought up in a home town—Portland, Maine—which he never ceased to love. As a senior at Bowdoin College he developed a fervent aspiration toward "future eminence in literature," and events promptly conspired to give him his wish. Bowdoin's trustees preserved him from the study of law by appointing him, at the age of eighteen, to a professorship of modern languages, and after three years of happy preparation abroad he returned to teach, first at Bowdoin, and then for eighteen years at Harvard. If he sometimes found teaching onerous, he was always successful at it, and never wearied of his material. As America's first poet-professor he was luckier than many since, in that for him there was "a complex and fruitful reaction between literary scholarship and literary creation." His house in Cambridge seemed to Emerson a palace; his domestic life, as Mr. Arvin says, "was one of almost pure felicity"; and his poetic reputation, beginning with *Voices of the Night* in 1839, grew steadily greater. He was translated, while living, into more than twenty languages, and on his death to the poets' corner of Westminster Abbey.

It was a lucky life, lived directly and serenely to its goal; and there were, as Mr. Arvin tells, other exceptional things about it. "Modern Languages" was not an established discipline in the 1820s, and Longfellow's teaching of European languages and literatures was thus a relatively fresh venture. He devised his own textbooks at Bowdoin; he was the first in America to offer a course in Goethe's *Faust*; his unprecedented collection of translations, *The Poets and Poetry of Eu-*

rope, was an enlightenment to all of literate America. In short, Longfellow's scholarly career had a creativeness which is now seldom remembered. Nor do we readily associate with Longfellow the unacademic gusto with which he approached his academic material: he learned his languages not in the schoolrooms and libraries of Europe, but in great measure by mixing in the daily life of people of all classes; his teaching was based on "the contagion of personal enthusiasm." Another aspect of the man was the way in which, as Henry James put it, "his 'European' culture and his native kept house together." Longfellow was, in his time, a major channel of European influence, and yet he appears never to have felt the least confusion as to where he belonged. One might begin to explain this by observing that nothing in Longfellow's American background was repressive or narrowing to a man of his temper; that he lacked the cold vanity and intellectuality necessary for any rational style of estrangement; and that his Europe was not ideas, politics, or a possible way of life, but a romantic literary experience. Nevertheless his cultural equilibrium remains a small marvel, and it is reflected in such a poem as "My Lost Youth," where Italian echoes, a classical reference, and a Lapland refrain encountered in German translation are made to blend perfectly with memories of a Maine boyhood.

Longfellow's emotional equilibrium was by no means perfect, and there were periods of intense private depression, anxiety, and hypochondria. One wonders how much these seizures may have proceeded from the unease of self-ignorance, from want of convictions or from that dread of vicissitude which accompanies a love of security. In contrast to Emily Dickinson, say, or Melville, Longfellow had no articulate inwardness, and such a poem as "The Fire of Driftwood" (of which Howard Nemerov has written so well) is atypical in its presentation of a live and nuanced psychology. In religion and morals, Longfellow was neither heretical nor orthodox but conventional, and he embraced a reduced and uncertain Christianity of "the deed, and not the creed" which cannot have been very fortifying against fear or trial. In any case, the poems of Longfellow seem the work of a man who has given all to the exercise of an authentic but limited talent and neglected to grapple with his own heart and mind. The huge work *Christus* is first of all an intellectual failure. "The Saga of King Olaf" is a stunning performance, as Mr. Arvin shows, but the delight in violence which informs it is never brought face to face, in any poem, with the pacifism of that equally fine poem, "The Arsenal at Springfield." Longfellow's last piece of writing, "The Bells of San Blas," is full of felicities, but troubles the reader with a sense not so much of conflict as of discontinuity of attitude. The first ten stanzas express nostalgic regret for the age of faith, but the last stanza (written, Mr. Arvin notes, after a lapse of time) is an abrupt affirmation of progress: "It is daybreak everywhere." Like Tennyson, Longfellow often juxtaposes two quite distinct voices, the one melancholy and desirous of repose, the other positive, edifying, and usually less convincing. "Though he believed in balance," William Charvat has observed, "he did not feel it." And Mr. Arvin makes the right objection to much of Longfellow's moralizing: it is not, as Poe thought, that the didactic has no place in poetry, but that Longfellow's moral lessons are likely to be hand-me-downs rather than trophies of "independent cogitation."

Had Mr. Arvin intended to stir up a Longfellow revival, he might have focused sharply, in his treatment of the work, on those shorter poems which seem most recoverable in view of current taste and reading habits. What he has done is even more interesting—to dismiss very little, and to allot his space with some regard to the pretensions of each work. If this makes for an honorable kind of slow going when ambitious failures are in question, it affords a sense of the whole oeuvre, acquaints us with the magnitude of the poet's role as Longfellow saw it, and challenges us to appreciate his successes in now disused poetic genera. A reviewer cannot comment in detail on commentaries, but Mr. Arvin is to be praised for not misapplying our prevalent criteria—ambiguity and so forth—to Longfellow; what he does is to look for the qualities in Longfellow which, fashionable or not, are worth noting or admiring, and the enquiry is both helpful and aesthetically enlarging. Longfellow emerges as a straightforward poet of mood, sentiment, and story, who was at his best "an accomplished, sometimes an exquisite, craftsman," who dealt in "states of feeling that remain this side of either ecstasy or despair," and whose better work is "worth preserving in some ideal anthology of verse of the second order." Mr. Arvin gives due attention to Longfellow's bold technical experiments in everything from free verse to the eight-stress line, finds "something almost Elizabethan in the range and freshness of Longfellow's work as a translator," and defensibly considers him the best American sonneteer of his century. One agrees, too, that Longfellow's storytelling is well-paced, varied, and thoroughly readable, especially in *Tales of a Wayside Inn*, and that we have to our cost forgotten his talent for humorous narrative. Among many acute passages in Mr. Arvin's critical chapters I particularly prize his observations on the translatableness of Longfellow's "limpid, uneccentric" language, on the poet's "use of literary allusion for purposes of metaphor" and on the associative structure of such poems as "The Jewish Cemetery at Newport."

In an epilogue, Mr. Arvin makes a valuable distinction among three kinds of popular poetry: folk, masscult, and demotic. Folk poetry is pre-literate or illiterate; masscult poetry is newspaper verse and the like; demotic poetry is work of genuine literary quality written in response to the emergence of "a very wide body of more or less educated but not sophisticated or exacting readers." That Longfellow consciously responded to such a public may be seen in his praise of "Songs that lowlier hearts feel," in the confident warmth with which he addresses his readers in the "Dedication" to *The Seaside and the Fireside*, and in his letters to G.W. Greene about "The Wreck of the Schooner Hesperus": "I have a great notion of working upon the people's feelings. I am going to have it printed on a sheet with a coarse picture on it. I desire a new sensation and a new set of critics...."

Contemporary Russia, with its new literate classes, its scarcity of cheap diversions, and its enormous editions of poetry, may be enjoying a kind of officially enforced demotic period; our own "great age of demotic poetry" is past, and Longfellow's reputation went with it. There is much in Longfellow—one has only to think of the powerful *Michael Angelo* or the subtly turned "Snow-Flakes"—which is not popular poetry in any sense, and could easily be more esteemed today. But what of the best of the bulk of his work? Have we no use whatever for the stirring ballad, the clear and modest lyric, the well-told tale? The effect of Mr. Arvin's study is to send us to Longfellow's high-demotic, with an awakened sense of its merits, and to convince us that it would be narrow and improvident to let it go.

Every Man His Own Eckermann

by Edmund Wilson

EDMUND WILSON: I'm delighted to hear about your new magazine.

THE VISITOR: We hope that it's going to be good.

WILSON: God knows that some such thing is needed. The disappearance of the *Times* Sunday book section at the time of the printers' strike only made us realize it had never existed. Apart from Norman Cousins's campaign for peace and an occasional article on popular science, the *Saturday Review* is interesting only for its reports on new phonograph records. And those quarterlies are still mostly wandering in the vast academic desert of the structure of *The Sound and the Fury*, the variants in the text of *Billy Budd*, and the religious significance of *The Great Gatsby*. But where did you get the money? Not from a foundation, I imagine.

THE VISITOR: That's where we were very lucky. We tried the foundations first, but of course there was nothing doing.

WILSON: The big ones, so far as I can see—in the literary and scholarly departments, at least—are run by second-rate professors who have found that they can make more money out of that kind of bureaucratic job than out of mediocre teaching. I've been trying for many years to get really good complete editions of the American classics printed—like the French Pléiade series, you know. When a publisher friend of mine who

has been trying to do something about it went to the Rocke-
feller Foundation, he was told that it would first be necessary
to have a study made in order to find out whether the books
were available—which everyone who has done any work in
this field could have told him at once they are not— and then
the foundation man remarked that there was really no point in
reprinting any author complete: Who ever read all of Shakespeare? At the Ford Foundation, he was told that the whole of
their cultural budget had been allotted to provide two planes
to fly over the Middle West, broadcasting educational pro-
grams. The people on these foundations do not seem to have
any competence to make judgments on the projects submitted
to them (I except the Guggenheim Foundation, which is an
older and quite different thing), and they feel free to formu-
late projects themselves in fields they know nothing about,
with no relevance to the applicants' aims. A middle-aged anthropologist who had devoted many years of his life to a group
of Australian aborigines or a tribe of Mexican Indians or
something of the sort was told, when he applied to one of the
foundations, that it had been discovered in their offices that
very little anthropological work had as yet been done on the
Turks, and that it might recommend him to investigate this
subject, of which he was totally ignorant. A scholar friend of
mine who is an expert on the numismatics of the Graeco-
Roman world had, when I last saw him, been trying without
success to get a grant which would enable him to do research
on the coinage of Alexander the Great—of special interest, it
seems, as the first really international coinage. I have just read
that he has been made chairman of the American School of
Classical Studies in Athens. I hear of nothing but such stupidi-
ties on the part of the big foundations.

I have just had a letter from the Ford Foundation inviting
me to recommend candidates—let me read it to you—for "a
one-year program designed to enable a limited number of

poets, novelists and short story writers to spend a year with professional resident theater companies. The intention of the program is to bring established writers in non-dramatic forms into formal association with the theater and, by acquainting them with stage problems and the requirements of dramatic writing, ultimately to improve the quality of plays and scripts available to American directors, actors and producers." What nonsense! A typical foundation project, obviously thought up by somebody who knows nothing about the theater. What are these prospective playwrights supposed to be actually doing? The way to learn about the theater is to have a play put on or to act in one, and a grant from the Ford Foundation can hardly help one much to do either. A man who really wants to write plays is sufficiently enamored of the theater to get into it at any cost. If a poet does not write plays, why encourage him to hang around theaters? There are some very good people here who are listed as having had grants, but what a far-fetched pretext for giving them money to work! In the case of the universities, I don't know whether the grants that they obtain from the foundations are for projects originated by the bureaucrats, which the university devotes to some other use, or whether the university, knowing how these things are done, dreams up some grandiose project which it knows will appeal to the foundation mind and then uses it for something else; but I have seen a certain amount of evidence that these subsidies do not always go for the purposes for which they were granted.

Well, tell me how you did get your subsidy.

THE VISITOR: It all comes from one backer.

WILSON: An old-fashioned patron?

THE VISITOR: Yes.

WILSON: You don't think he'll interfere with you?

THE VISITOR: I don't see how he can. He's unshockable—about politics or religion or art or sex or anything. He doesn't want his name made public, but he's a cultivated European who married a rich American woman. She died and left him all her money, and he doesn't know what to do with it. He's a collector of various things, but his collections are now practically complete, and are beginning in fact to bore him. He says that, first of all, he would like to see a review that he himself can read, and, second, that a country as big as this and as powerful as we are now supposed to be has enough nearly literate people to make it perhaps important to establish a cultural journal which will not have to worry about money and so will be free to set its own standards and to get only first-rate writers who are allowed to say anything they please. He himself was something of a figure in the cultural life of his country before the Russians took over.

WILSON: Won't he want to contribute himself?

THE VISITOR: He comes from a country with a minority language only spoken by a few hundred thousand people. He has always read English but he doesn't write it. German was his second language.

WILSON: One of those Baltic barons?

THE VISITOR: I'm not allowed to tell.

WILSON: Well, I congratulate you!—You say "cultural journal." So you won't be dealing only with books.

THE VISITOR: No, with all the arts—and that's what I wanted to ask you about. You've written so much about literature but not much about painting and music. We wondered if you wouldn't contribute some opinions about graphic and musical subjects.

WILSON: Gladly: I know nothing whatever about them.

THE VISITOR: But in the Twenties you used to do articles on concerts and exhibitions.

WILSON: Oh, that was in the days when I was cultural man-of-all-work for *The New Republic*. I wrote about everything from burlesque shows and circuses to Stravinsky and Georgia O'Keeffe. I'd never dare to write such stuff today.

THE VISITOR: An informal interview, perhaps.

WILSON: That's what I thought you meant.

THE VISITOR: I'm sure you must have some ideas on current tendencies in the musical and artistic worlds.

WILSON: I never think much in terms of tendencies even in the literary world. I have preferences in music and painting, of course, but there wouldn't be any point in enumerating, for example, my favorite painters. In my case, such preferences would be of no interest. If I should say that I like Edwin Dickinson but don't very much like Rouault, it would be like announcing in public that I like shad but don't like lobster. In order to talk critically about an art, you have to have some inside knowledge of it, and as I'm neither a musician nor a painter even in an amateur way, I don't really know how those things are done, so, in any technical sense, I don't know what these artists are doing.

THE VISITOR: It would be interesting to hear your preferences.

WILSON: Not for painters or musicians, I'm afraid. But if you want some unauthoritative opinions, here goes. There's one great phenomenon of modern painting about which I seem to be in a minority of one. That's Picasso. I can't really feel much interest in him. Of course, I see the brilliance of his work, and even at times the beauty. I'm willing to believe that Picasso is

the greatest draftsman since Raphael—that he's a prodigy
of inventiveness, "resourcefulness," virtuosity, variety, all that.
And yet somehow the whole thing bores me. I can't help feeling that the man himself is shallow. The deliberate ugliness of
his women that are seen simultaneously in fishlike full-face
and profile seems to me in its way just as facile as the pathos
and charm of the acrobats that he was doing in his early period, or the cubism that he played with and abandoned. He
goes on doing one thing after the other without ever becoming
more interesting. It's all on the same level! His idea of tragic
bitterness at the time of the Spanish Civil War! He could only
make Franco grotesque and humanly unbelievable, and those
horses with tongues like spikes and eyes like little dots on the
sides of their heads—that he said represented the Spanish
people—and those caricatured classical women with their
thick necks and wooden faces and their fingers and toes like
sausages—you can't imagine them suffering anguish. Picasso
was much more interested in his cleverness in putting over
women and horses that looked like that than in anything con-
nected with Franco. You know that popular print that belongs
to the Guernica period: the little girl holding a candle and con-
fronting the monstrous Minotaur? Once years ago my wife
was going to buy it as a Christmas present for me, but was dis-
suaded by Clement Greenberg, the art critic, who assured her
that I'd very soon get bored with it. So I bought it for myself
and hung it in my office, and Greenberg's prediction was cor-
rect. I usually enjoy the horrific, but I couldn't believe in that
Minotaur, and eventually I gave it away. Put Picasso beside
Goya and he's nowhere. In Goya you do feel the horror—a
desperate and tortured contempt—of the cruelties of war and
the Inquisition, of Saturn devouring his children. And his
drawings are dark and corrosive, they leave a scar on the
mind, whereas—in spite of his calculated outrageousness—
Picasso merely startles and amuses. I never get tired of Goya,

who is, on the whole, I suppose, the artist that I find most congenial.

I have always had a very strong taste for the satirical and the rather sinister; and I am under the impression—which artists tell me makes no sense—that I am much more sensitive to line than to color. I like things to be rather dry and drawn sharply instead of fluently. I particularly admire Degas, and Matisse means very little to me. My first great admirations were Hogarth and Dürer—I had them up on my walls in my youth. Then I discovered Callot, who is of course a lesser artist but has a special personal interest for me. I was stationed in France during the First World War near Nancy in Lorraine, where Callot was born, and when the city was threatened by the Germans, an old print dealer there got out and set up shop in the town where I was. I bought from him a number of Callot prints, some made from the original blocks, and a copy of the eighteenth-century engraving copied from Callot's most popular plate, *La Tentation de Saint-Antoine*. These stood me in good stead. They fell in with my mood of those years and they gave me a certain support. I had some of the series of *Désastres de la Guerre*—which inspired Goya's series—and I took acrid satisfaction in the irony and objectivity of Callot's point of view. I still like to have these prints around me. Later on I got Lieure's *Catalogue* of Callot, which beautifully reproduces in many fascicules the whole of his engraved and other work. It is fascinating. It seems to unroll the whole life of the seventeenth century: wars, fairs, landscapes, views of the cities, beggars, Commedia dell'Arte actors, the ceremonies and fetes of the court—with the people seen as sharp tiny figures, almost on the scale of insects. It is characteristic of Callot that when he gives us a closer view of them, they are likely to be less satisfactory: their features are not so clearly stamped as these prickly little midgelike figures.

I like picture books in general of the comic or fantastic

kind: Gilray, Rowlandson, Fuseli, Spitzweg, Cruikshank, Phiz, Edward Lear, Beardsley, Toulouse-Lautrec, George du Maurier, Phil May, Max Beerbohm, Sem, Max Ernst, Marc Chagall, Peggy Bacon, Saul Steinberg, Leonard Baskin, Edward Gorey—to mention people of very different magnitudes. But a would-be ironist that I do not like is that half-baked Belgian, Ensor. I believe that Sem, the great French caricaturist, is a much underrated artist. He is one of those people that the French consign to an inferior category —like Yvette Guilbert, who was certainly one of the great French artists of her time, but who, when she went back to France in the Twenties, having greatly extended her range during the years she had lived in America, was still never taken seriously in Paris, where they spoke of her rather disdainfully as "*une chanteuse de café chantant.*" So Forain is taken seriously, is supposed to belong to legitimate art, though he is certainly a second-rate artist and apparently a detestable person—Sem's caricatures of Forain are interesting from this point of view—whereas Sem is somehow still a mere journalist, though he is actually a far more interesting and a more distinguished artist. He had a whole very remarkable artistic development: from his earliest albums which he published in the Eighties, of old-fashioned caricatures of the prominent people in the French provincial cities—who subscribed, I suppose, to these albums—to his wonderful mature work, in which the whole social world of Paris is presented year after year, with its changing fashions in costume and restaurants and dances and sports. And even in this later work there is a striking constant development: there is even an advance in draftsmanship between the album which shows all his Parisian characters mad about dancing the Tango and the one in which they are dancing the Black Bottom. The one about the Black Bottom contains some of Sem's best work. He is a master at showing action. How would Elsa Maxwell and the Aga Khan and Barry Wall and Cécile Sorel disport themselves in wildly succumbing to the spirit of the Black Bottom? Everyone will dance it differently, and the album is a tumult of movement. And everybody is dressed characteristically. Sem was a contemporary of Sargent, and he has something of Sargent's virtuosity with fine fabrics and well-cut garments: the silk hats and smart clothes of the men, the great cloaks and long skirts of the ladies in the era before skirts were lifted. There is never any touch of idealization. Sem's art is astringent but rarely brutal, and the people are usually enjoying themselves. Proust's favorite, Robert de Montesquiou, was also a favorite of Sem's, and it is curious to compare Sem's caricatures of him with the character of Proust's Charlus, to which Montesquiou is supposed to have contributed. Charlus is temperamental and uncomfortable, humiliated, venomous, doomed, whereas Montesquiou according to Sem is always having the time of his life, dining with his friend Yturri, who adores him, or strutting through a recitation of his poems to an audience of delighted ladies. I don't know why the people who write about Proust don't illustrate their books with Sem's caricatures. He and Proust knew one another, and they were dealing with the same society. It is said that Sem used to stay up till all hours in fashionable restaurants waiting for the moment when some fashionable lady would drop her social mask—which seems to me very Proustian. But Sem rarely aims to degrade as Proust so often does. His drawings have often a peculiar beauty—those of the actress Brandes, with her flat yellow pompadour, her skull-like face and the gestures, at once sinuous and angular, of her long-boned body and arms; the old Rothschild couple, at sunset, walking along the abandoned beach, she moving ahead with her positive umbrella and her salient determined chin, he strolling behind with his half-closed eyes, his black suit and his long white dundrearies; and even the dandiacal figure of the professional decadent Jean Lorrain—with whom Proust once fought a duel—vulgarly precious and weakly supercilious, his fingers loaded with rings.

THE VISITOR: Daumier?

WILSON: For some reason I don't enjoy Daumier nearly so much as some other people that I know are his inferiors as artists. I think that the trouble is that a kind of classical sculpture somehow blunts the effect of his satire. Gavarni I don't like at all—it's a proof of the Goncourts' dubious taste that they make such a fuss about him. I suppose that on account of his being so unimaginative they thought he was naturalistic. The drawings of Henri Monnier are feeble enough in this satirical vein, but his little one-act dramas or dialogues are really biting *eaux-fortes* in prose. They anticipate Flaubert and Maupassant. Well, people tell me—though I don't think it's entirely true—that I mainly go to pictures for the qualities of literature, that what I really like are illustrations.

THE VISITOR: But a good deal of the work of Picasso has also illustrational interest.

WILSON: Yes: he turns out innumerable albums, but I never buy these albums. I look through them in the houses of friends. — Oh, I forgot to mention George Grosz: perhaps the very greatest of the satirical artists—at least as great as Hogarth. There has lately been an excellent film made from his drawings and paintings, which brings out the concentrated life that Grosz has put into all those middle-class German faces: their brutality, meanness, stupidity, complacency, debauchery, cruelty, coarseness. I do not remember anything by Picasso that is brought into so sharp a focus. The faces of all these creatures, no matter how brute-like they are, have expressions of the fiercest intensity: they reflect the intensity of the artist. And Grosz, too, is a master draftsman. The stock thing to say about him, after he came to America in 1932, was that his work was no longer so interesting; but this was not at all true. He had a straight non-satirical side, which he mainly developed in the United States: the sand dunes, the nude figures, the portraits of friends, all as solidly constructed as Dürers. And when he went back to satire at the time of Hitler, his Nazi butchers and miserable "Stickmen" were as powerful as anything he had done in his youth and were remarkable for a new use of color. It is true that when he first came to this country, he somewhat relented in his harshness, so that his work seemed less characteristic. There was a German admiration for America that was not merely chic as in France but was based on the obvious features that Germany had had in common with us: energetic activity, mechanical skill, urban building, and middle-class comfort. I had never really understood how far this admiration had gone in George Grosz's case till I asked him once what he thought of American painting. He said that he didn't think much of it but that American commercial art was something new in the world, which did interest him. It created a whole ideal of the desirable and attainable life: handsome men and beautiful women, with their spic-and-span smiling children, all eating the most excellent food, traveling in the smoothest-running cars, basking and getting tanned on the most enjoyable beaches, housewives relieved of drudgery, husbands coming home from the office and relaxing in adjustable chairs while the loving but comradely wives bring them a reviving martini. It had never occurred to me before that the pictures in our advertisements might be of interest to subsequent civilizations, like Greek statues and Cretan murals. They certainly made a startling contrast to George Grosz's conception of life in Berlin, but since I did not much believe in the ideal they depicted and thought that the realities of American life offered plenty of subjects for satire, I was surprised to discover that George was more or less delighted with America. In his account of his return to Germany, it is plain that he is full of pride at exhibiting himself as an American. He said that he bought for the occasion one of the most ostentatious of those gaudy American ties that were popular a few years ago—he would never have worn one in New York. The same thing seems to have happened in the case of Kurt Weill. Behind the revolutionary satire of *Mahagonny*, for example, which is supposed to take place in the United States, where neither he nor Bert Brecht had ever been, you feel an admiration for America, and when Weill did come over here, it was astonishing to find that he was able to get quite away from that German turbidity and sullenness, and to turn out such pretty poignancies as *September Song*, which appealed so success-fully to the American taste, and some of the numbers in *One Touch of Venus*.

In any case, George Grosz had swung himself quite out of the orbit of the great European central Paris market, which had operated with such shrewdness and assiduity in building up Picasso and the rest. It seems to me that he and Chelishchev—and please *don't* spell it Tchelitchew, though he let it go that way himself: he said that he did not sign his pictures, nobody else could have painted them—Chelishchev and George Grosz, it seems to me, were always at a disadvantage in not belonging to the Paris club. Chelishchev was a brilliant painter, who began as something of an imitator of Picasso but arrived at an originality less extroverted, rather morbid but extremely imaginative—with his pathetic gallery of freaks, his trees that turn into children and his anatomical paintings of desquamated human heads, all in queer iridescent harlequin colors that it seems to me no one but a Russian, with a Russian's love of gorgeousness and lack of chastened taste, would ever have thought of combining. And there is a Russian ingenuity that goes with these rather garishly assorted colors. Those deceptive paintings of Chelishchev that seem to be trees or portraits but turn out to conceal other things have a kinship with the novels of Nabokov, who loves to perform the same kind of tricks, and to juxtapose gemmy colors, as both are very much in the tradition of the precious mechanical peacock that Catherine the Great gave Potyomkin and those very fancy Easter eggs that rich Russians used to order from Fabergé. I suppose there's something Byzantine about it. The many colored vestments of the old Greek Orthodox Church, with their Fabergé gold and silver, make the same sort of impression on me. It may well be that Pavel Chelishchev was actually, as he seemed to believe, the greatest Russian painter since the ikon-makers. He used to say that Peter the Great had destroyed the tradition of Russian paintings by putting the ikon-makers out of business, and that he had been appointed to revive it. In any case, Chelishchev, like George Grosz, came to the United States, and neither of them has ever attained to the same international currency as the members of the organized surrealist group, all of whom it seems to me—unless Dali—were very much inferior to them. But they did not belong to a group and were never the darlings of the dealers.

THE VISITOR: I should imagine that you don't care much for abstract painting.

WILSON: In the matter of the abstract painters, I have only a coarse jest: they might be useful as designers of linoleum if they were capable of the necessary discipline.

THE VISITOR: You were speaking of Kurt Weill. Have you similar prejudices in music?

WILSON: I'm afraid that my taste in music is influenced as much by my interest in the drama as my interest in the graphic arts is influenced by their literary content. To me, such composers as Verdi and Wagner are primarily great dramatists, and I have had a good deal of pleasure in getting complete recordings of their operas and following their libretti line by line, which

since I'm not able to read the scores and since you can't really
follow them in the opera house, I've never been able to do
before. Also, *Boris Godunov*. When I first saw it at the Metro-
politan and tried to make sense of the Italian libretto, I
couldn't understand what it was all about. It was only when
I read Pushkin's play and got to know more about Russia
that I could see how terrifically dramatic it was. Musorgsky's
libretto, which I had never seen till I got a recent Soviet
recording, is one of the best ever written. Musorgsky wrote
this himself. He based it on Pushkin's tragedy—which is not
one of his most successful works: an attempt to write a Russian *Macbeth*—and converted it into a masterpiece. He added
elements from Russian folk music—like the ballad of the
Siege of Kazan. The Soviet version has restored it to Musorgsky's original arrangement. The Idiot is given his proper
importance in the scene where he says to Boris: "The nasty
boys took my kopeck. Give orders to have their throats cut as
you cut the little Tsarevich's throat"; and then he reappears at
the end. They sometimes in Western productions have it end
with the death of Boris, but this is all wrong. Musorgsky had
made it end with the army of the rebellion marching off and
the Idiot left behind, sitting alone on the stage, as the snow begins to fall. He sings again his ominous song that he has sung
after his scene with Boris:

> *Flow, flow, bitter tears*
> *Weep, weep, Christian souls.*
> *Soon the darkness will fall,*
> *A darkness extremely dark,*
> *Which we shall not be able to see through.*
> *Woe, Woe, Russia.*
> *Weep, Russian people,*
> *Hungry people!*

—with its little twitching accompaniment—I hope you don't mind my singing. This is one of the greatest moments in opera. (It could hardly have been done that way when Stalin was alive.) But everything in Musorgsky is dramatic. Compare the sound of the bells in *Boris* and in *Khovanshchina*—in the first, they are mocking at Boris, evidently making him uneasy, at the same time that they are celebrating his coronation; in the second, they are pounding an assertion of power. And the *Songs and Dances of Death*: the dialogue between Death and the mother of the dying child, with the spine-chilling voice of Death singing a lullaby while the mother grows more and more frantic, the peasant dying in the snowstorm while the voice of Death sings him the trepak.

THE VISITOR: How do you feel about contemporary opera?

WILSON: I very much admire Britten—though I am told by musical friends that I shouldn't admire him so much. He, too, has the dramatic sense to a degree that is very rare. The interludes in *Peter Grimes* that so intensify the drama of the action, the shadowy buildup of *The Turn of the Screw*, with its children's voices and nursery jingles that are always made shadowy, too. Britten's *Turn of the Screw* is altogether an original creation, quite distinct from Henry James's story. Menotti of course, too, has the dramatic instinct highly developed; but he is sometimes more a man of the theater than a first-rate musical artist. Berg's *Wozzeck* and *Lulu*, too—though I've only heard the latter on records—are most effective in their creepy way. *Lulu* is a very strange performance. Berg sets out to turn into opera the whole of Frank Wedekind's long play in two parts that deals with the destructive career of the simpleminded but irresistible "*Erdgeist*" Lulu, and through hours of grayest recitative the more or less repulsive characters discuss their sordid affairs, financial as well as artistic and amorous. The play itself is always in danger of becoming unintentionally funny—so it presents a considerable challenge—but Berg has put into it, it seems to me, more real pathos than Wedekind was capable of, and at the end the terrible shriek of the Jack the Ripper scene has been led up to with as much suspense and comes with as much horror as the murder of the wife in *Wozzeck*, with the ripples spreading out on the water when the murderer throws his knife into the pond. I wonder whether the monochrome of *The Turn of the Screw*—not particularly characteristic of Britten—doesn't derive from the tonelessness of *Wozzeck*. The nursery rhymes of the children and the boy's piano exercise are flattened and deprived of their melodic fullness like the song of the woman at the window and the military march in *Wozzeck*. It is all like a discolored photograph—very effective in its melancholy ghostly way, but it makes one long for something more ringing.

THE VISITOR: Have you heard Schoenberg's *Moses and Aron*?

WILSON: Only on records, again. It is impressive, but, in spite of its leaning on Wagner, it did not seem to me very dramatic—though I'm told that the orgy of the Golden Calf, which needs a ballet, of course, is quite terrific on the stage. But what a disagreeable orgy, so full of reminders of death!—though this is, of course, just what Schoenberg intends. The Wagnerian romanticism that Schoenberg began with, as his later method developed, was reduced to more and more of a starvation diet; and I felt about *Moses and Aron* that it was too moralistic and didactic—very much a lugubrious monologue of the somber and stern Jewish master, who is never to arrive in the Promised Land. Moses goes up on the mountain and is handed the laws of the twelve-tone row. It takes him some time to grasp them, and while he has been away, the people have been getting dissatisfied. They are longing to dance and to sing, and Aron—who is somebody like Stravinsky or Bartók or Hin-

demith, who is weak enough to make use of melody—agrees
to let them have their fun. At the end of the Golden Calf rev-
elry, Moses comes down from the mountain and is deeply
shocked by what has been going on. The Golden Calf vanishes,
and the people complain that their *joie de vivre* has been taken
from them. Moses rebukes Aron, who has been disloyal to his
leader by giving them "*das Bild*" and "*das Wunder*" instead of
waiting for Moses to bring his "*Gedanke*," which transcends
these meretricious attractions. Aron defends himself on the
ground that ordinary people are only able to comprehend
a part of the all-inclusive "*Gedanke*." "Shall I debase *der
Gedanke*?" cries Moses—that is, abandon the serial system.
He smashes the Tables of the Law and begs God to relieve him
of his mission. For the very queer and arrogant last scene,
Schoenberg never wrote the music. His difficulties and doubts
about it are shown in certain passages of his letters. It was as
if he, too, had broken his tables, as if he, too, were becoming
discouraged, were losing his grip on his mission. But he had
written the libretto for this scene, and here Aron-Stravinsky is
brought in chains, and Moses-Schoenberg bawls him out for
stooping to please the people instead of consecrating his gifts
to the *Gottesgedanke*. "Shall we kill him?" the soldiers ask.
"No," says Moses. "Set him free, and let him live if he can." But
Aron is by this time so crushed by shame that when the soldiers release him, he falls down dead—which is not the case in
the Bible, where he continues to cooperate with Moses and
take orders directly from God.

THE VISITOR: What do you think of twelve-tone music in
general?

WILSON: I can't follow it, so I don't really know. But I've found
it reassuring to learn that accomplished musicians can't follow
it either—that is, simply to listen to it without a score. I was
talking about it the other day with one of the most distin-

guished American conductors, and one who is particularly
notable for his catholicity of taste. I asked in what way the serial system was an improvement on music that was simply
atonal. He said that it had two advantages. *One*, that it gave to
the analysts of scores and the writers of program notes more
scope for their technical explaining and made their explaining
more necessary; and *Two*, that a man like Schoenberg, so exacting and puritanical, having completely made hay of the
conventional harmonies, felt constrained to impose on himself
a difficult gratuitous discipline. Debussy had not felt the need
of any such theoretical structure, and Webern, though he followed Schoenberg's system, could have achieved his effects
without it. But the serial system has, in any case, by this time
become something of a cult. I'm told that in the schools of
music, the Schoenberg technique is now so much the thing
that the students have to withstand a strong pressure, and
even to risk something like ostracism, if they don't want to
become twelve-toners. A friend of mine who has seen a good
deal of these students tells me that it is almost like the pressure of a homosexual group—though he didn't mean to imply
that there was any connection between homosexuality and
serial music. Except, of course, that they're both *culs de sac*. It
strikes me that—in America, at least—the composers are the
most ingrown group of any in the major arts. Their audience is
so limited, and it is almost as if, finding themselves doomed to
this, they take pride in defying the neglect of them by making
it more limited still. They feel safer in the Kafka-esque burrow
of the dark and hidden twelve-tone row.

But I'm afraid that the Anglo-Saxons are no longer a
musical people—though they seem to have been in the past.
Shakespeare is full of music, and the poetry up through the
seventeenth century continues to show the influence of music
to a degree that you don't find today. It may be that the
Cromwellian attack on the Church and the theater and on gai-

ety in general blasted music so it never recovered. In any case, the Anglo-Saxon world has not for several centuries been musical. In Germany and Italy and Russia, the people were always singing and playing on some instrument or other. But I don't think we have much music in us. Prokofiev, for example, may not have been a great composer, but he was certainly full of music. So was Richard Strauss, who was certainly not a great composer. We have no such composers as this. Of course our popular music is brilliant, and it goes all over the world. But a good deal of it has been derived from materials provided by the Negroes, with their supreme African sense of rhythm, and much of the best of it has been written by Jews. I don't know why the Jews should be so musical. Perhaps they brought their love of music from Russia and the German-speaking countries, and they could cultivate music in the synagogue at a time when a Jew was not free to cultivate the plastic arts, and when his full self-expression in literature was still hampered by difficulties of language.

It seems to me, besides, that the problem of a market has affected non-popular music more perhaps than it has done even painting. Music is not a parasitic art, but in order really to flourish, it seems to need to be supported by some well-established institution that will enable it to reach a large audience: the theater, the Church, the dance. The symphony orchestras can keep it alive, but they cannot—even by way of recordings—make the music of the concert hall a part of the life of a people. The dramatic element is very important. Aside from church music and opera, you find that even in concert-hall music Beethoven was a one-man drama, as was Brahms in his quieter way, and Richard Strauss, when he was not doing operas, was composing his programmatic "tone-poems," which could not be more theatrical. A Menotti can make money by writing for the stage, a Copland by writing for ballet or the movies, but a non-dramatic composer, unless he has private means, has to depend on grants from foundations or get a job in the music department of some university. How great would be Stravinsky's reputation or how widely would his work be played, if he had not in his early career made connections with Dyagilev and been able to go on writing ballets all his life. His nontheatrical works are as delightful as everything else he writes but they are only very rarely played—you have to get them on records.

THE VISITOR: You do admire Stravinsky?

WILSON: Tremendously. Unlike Picasso, Stravinsky *has* meant a good deal to me—more than any other contemporary artist in any nonliterary art. It is inspiring for any kind of craftsman to have the spectacle of such a sustained career— the artist always himself and always doing something different, but always doing everything intensely with economy, perfect craftsmanship, and style—so different from Picasso's diffuseness that sometimes seems almost mere doodling. Stravinsky has kept going through his eighties with such tireless pertinacity and vivacity that I feel he has helped me to keep going. I'm not in the least religious, but I think it's significant and admirable that Stravinsky should begin every day with a prayer.

—Well, I guess that's enough. When people get to talking about subjects that they don't really know inside out, you are likely to get a combination of banalities, naivetés, and what I love to have my critics call "gross blunders," and I expect I've been guilty of all of them. I hope that I haven't made Sem seem more important than Michelangelo—or given you the impression that I haven't in the past very much admired Schoenberg.

THE VISITOR: Thank you very much.—Now, what doo yoo theenk of thees keend of myooseec?

A prolonged even whistle is heard.

WILSON: It doesn't sound eeree or loopee enough for electronic myooseec.

THE VISITOR: Eelectroneec? Noo: Eelectrooloox—a keend of myooseec freequeentlee heerd een thee oordeenaree Ameereecan hoosehoold.

WILSON: Yes: eet soonds veeree fameeliar. Noo, tell mee, what are yoo going too call yoor magazeen?

THE VISITOR: The seem neem: Eelectroloox, and thee poorpose weel bee the seem.

WILSON: Woon't yoo reeveel, pleese?

THE VISITOR: Eeee—eesee, eeesee does eet. Thees weel geeve yoo soom ideee of the keend of mateereeal that wee are hooping too coollect and preesent.

The sound suddenly ceases. Wilson awakes. The maid has stopped the vacuum cleaner in order to empty its contents.